Personnel Management in Merchant Ships

Personnel Management in Merchant Ships

BY

D. H. MOREBY, *Master Mariner, Extra Master*

SENIOR LECTURER IN SHIP MANAGEMENT
PLYMOUTH COLLEGE OF TECHNOLOGY

1966
THE QUEEN'S AWARD
TO INDUSTRY 1966

PERGAMON PRESS

OXFORD · LONDON · EDINBURGH · NEW YORK
TORONTO · SYDNEY · PARIS · BRAUNSCHWEIG

Pergamon Press Ltd., Headington Hill Hall, Oxford
4 & 5 Fitzroy Square, London W.1

Pergamon Press (Scotland) Ltd., 2 & 3 Teviot Place, Edinburgh 1

Pergamon Press Inc., 44–01 21st Street, Long Island City,
New York 11101

Pergamon of Canada Ltd., 207 Queen's Quay West, Toronto 1

Pergamon Press (Aust.) Pty. Ltd., 19a Boundary Street,
Rushcutters Bay, Sydney, N.S.W. 2011, Australia

Pergamon Press S.A.R.L., 24 rue des Écoles, Paris 5ᵉ

Vieweg & Sohn GmbH, Burgplatz 1, Braunschweig

Printed in Great Britain by A. Wheaton & Co., Exeter

08 012992 7 (flexicover)
08 012993 5 (hard cover)

1505044

Contents

Preface

THE human problems aboard merchant ships are much the same, no matter what the nationality of the ships or the crews. This book refers to British legislation, but readers sailing under other flags should have no difficulty in relating the situations to their own legislation.

I am grateful to the British Shipping Federation, the National Union of Seamen and the Merchant Navy and Airline Officers' Association for all the help and information so freely given to me. I should also like to thank the Honourable Company of Master Mariners, the Mercantile Marine Service Association and the Radio Officers' Union for supplying me with information for this book.

My deepest gratitude, however, goes to the three men who wrote parts of this book: to J. Andrew Davies, Extra Master, Dip.Ed., Dip.P.L. (Birmingham), for the chapter on Education; to Alfred E. Carver, Extra Master, M.Phil., for the chapter on Nautical Education; and to S. Starks, A.M.I.B.M., A.I.W.S.P., for the chapter on Work Study. I feel I am indeed fortunate to work with such competent and helpful men.

I should also acknowledge, with thanks, the permission given to me by the Controller of Her Majesty's Stationery Office to include extracts from various Government Reports in this book.

This acknowledgement must not be taken to imply that any of the persons or organizations mentioned above necessarily agree with all the views expressed in this book. The responsibility for all the views and statements made throughout this book is entirely mine.

D. H. M.

Foreword

In an era of modernization and great change David Moreby and his co-authors have produced a very readable and constructive book on the many factors relating to the seafaring environment.

It is not, as the title would suggest, restricted to an exercise in Personnel Management—although there are some very valuable chapters on this subject—but ranges over such subjects as human relations, education, management techniques, to the qualities required for leadership, all issues with which the Association has been closely identified. It also emphasizes the need for the "whole man" approach, which is to be highly commended.

In all, it is a book that should be read by every Merchant Navy officer and, indeed, by those concerned with sea-going personnel.

D. S. Tennant, c.b.e.
General Secretary,
Merchant Navy and Airline Officers' Association

Men at sea live in a close community. This gives an opportunity and a need for exercising skills in personnel management which are probably unique.

The industry is giving a great deal of thought to the basic human problems of seafarers: their hopes and fears; what helps them to develop their full potentiality; what encourages them to give of their best. Positive steps are being taken to assist officers, petty officers, and shore management, to understand these problems.

This book is, therefore, timely. It is comprehensive and easily read. No one is asked to accept or agree with every point made—I do not do so myself. But they are all important in arousing thought on a vital subject.

Ford I. Geddes, m.b.e.
Chairman,
The British Shipping Federation

CHAPTER 1

Work and Status

THE aim of this book is to help seamen understand other seamen.

Each one of us at sea is a whole, complete person. Each has his own personality, his own strengths and his own weaknesses. Certain personnel-handling techniques may suit one man and yet appear to be completely false when adopted by another. No man should try to mould his whole character on the principles laid down in this book. Instead, this book should be used as a guide towards better personnel management at sea and a man should only adopt those techniques which are best suited to his personality.

If we are to understand others we should first examine the reasons why people work. All of us work for the same reasons; the only difference between one man and another being that each has his own order of priorities. One man, for example, may search for a job which will bring him the highest income while another may search for security; one man may seek satisfaction while another seeks status.

Before examining the reasons why an individual works we should consider why a whole community works. Humans work for one simple reason and that is a living must be wrung from the earth. The earth gives only raw materials—mineral and vegetable —which usually have to be processed in some way before they can be consumed or used by humans. A country which has an abundance of raw materials will gear her economy to them and her people will become farmers or miners. A country without raw materials will have to develop a manufacturing economy; she will have to make things which other countries want to buy, and her people will become factory workers and salesmen. All people, however, whether they be farmers or factory workers, miners or salesmen, sell part of themselves when they go to work; they sell their physical or mental efforts for the wages they are paid.

Britain has a manufacturing economy and as long as she earns foreign money by selling goods abroad she can buy food and raw materials from other countries. The food, of course, is needed to feed her people, while the raw materials provide the basis for factory work. As long as markets for manufactured goods last, there will be work for all, but if the markets abroad were blocked and the supplies of raw materials dried up, then many people in Britain would be out of work.

In order to earn foreign money, Britain sells "visible" exports, such as motor cars, machinery and whisky, and "invisible" exports such as insurance, banking and transport services. One important invisible export is the freight earned by British ships. A British ship may, for example, take a cargo of machinery from the United Kingdom to Buenos Aires and, after discharge, may be chartered to carry a cargo of grain to Hamburg. From there she may take steel products to Lagos and from there a cargo of cocoa to New York. For each of these voyages the ship will be paid freight in foreign currency and, as hundreds of British ships may be engaged in trades similar to the one described, it becomes apparent that British ships earn for Britain many millions of pounds each year. Various estimates indicate that British ships earn about £170 million per year in foreign exchange and, if Britain had no merchant ships of her own, then not only would she lose this revenue, but she would have to pay out a further £300 million to foreign shipowners to carry her imports and exports. Every man taking part in the shipping industry can, therefore, feel proud that he is helping Britain to this extent.

The main point to grasp is that in a country with a manufacturing economy such as in Britain, industry supports the community. The young, the old and the sick must all be cared for. The services which are often taken for granted—posts, police, transport and the removal of rubbish, to name just a few—must all be paid for. The country must be defended and the children educated. Who pays for all this but industry? And industry is not just "the bosses". Industry is a partnership of all workers, each doing his separate and distinct job. Whether a man works ashore or at sea, he is a partner in industry and is helping to pay for all the social services. A man should also remember that, as a partner in industry, more and more will be demanded of him with each year that passes.

In forty years from now the population of the world will almost have doubled and all these people will have to be fed. The earth will not change in size, so this increase in population simply means that people will have to work harder and more efficiently. High productivity calls for increased efficiency all round. The machines which are looked upon today as the most efficient appliances for speeding a vessel on her way will be old fashioned in twenty years time. Already, we have high-speed turbine pumps in tankers and containers in cargo ships by means of which vessels can be turned round in hours, rather than in days or weeks. Port turn-round time will be reduced even more in the future. Many seamen will be surprised to learn that the record for loading a ship was set as far back as 1958 when 12,500 tons of ore were loaded in 16 minutes.

Not only merchant shipping but every other branch of industry is working at a considerably faster pace than it was a few years ago. Take, for example, the travelling salesman (or company representative, as he is called today). No longer does he move leisurely from call to call with ample time for telling jokes. Today he is supplied with a powerful motor car and a portable dictaphone and instead of calling on three or four firms per day he may have to make twelve calls and dictate his letters onto tape in between. Any man who feels he is rushed at sea should question workers ashore in order to find that he is subjected to the same conditions and pressures as everyone else in industry.

Now that we have looked, briefly, at industry as a whole, we can examine the personal reasons for working.

All men work for the same reasons, but as was mentioned earlier, individuals adopt different orders of priorities. There are only four reasons why people work. They work for money, security, satisfaction, and status.

One reason for working is for the money we earn. We use this money to meet the daily needs of food, shelter and clothing for ourselves and our families, and to raise our standard of living. A fair day's pay for a fair day's work is a healthy outlook, but to work only for the money it brings in is unhealthy. We need only think, for example, of some men who work in remote regions of the world under onerous conditions; they earn very high wages, but as soon as they return to civilization the money they earned is wasted—and the rate at which it is wasted is often accelerated by "female acquaintances".

Another reason for work is our need for security. Under this heading we get to the very root of group behaviour and discipline. There are two types of security—financial and social—and a man can only get both by working.

Financial security comes from being trained for a particular job and from working at it for some time. A man who has been with a particular firm for many years knows that, in return for the service he has given, he will have a job for the following month, the following year or for the following ten years. He can plan and budget accordingly. He can buy a house on a mortgage or a car on hire-purchase. On the other hand, a man who is forever changing his job does not enjoy the same financial security—one day he may be at sea, the next selling paint and a month later selling insurance. This man cannot know with any certainty where he will be a year hence nor what his salary will be; he cannot budget for the future.

Work, however, is a social activity and by contributing to the welfare of his society (for that is what a man does when he works) a man is accepted by that society. A man likes to feel that he "belongs" and does not like to feel that he is a social outcast. The great evil of unemployment is not that families go short of food, clothing or luxuries, but that a man out of work feels that he is rejected by society. He does not feel that he "belongs" to society while he is on the dole and many a man has taken a job at a rate of pay lower than his weekly dole simply to regain this feeling of "belonging".

This need to feel that he belongs makes a man seek the approval of his fellows. If his society recognizes conquest, he will engage in aggressive behaviour; if it recognizes wealth, he will make sacrifices in order to entertain lavishly; and if it recognizes tough drunkenness, he will engage in that sort of behaviour. Take, for example, the young cadet on arrival at his first foreign port. He may really want to visit local places of interest yet, because the men with whom he goes ashore are thirsty and want to satisfy certain sensual desires, he sees nothing other than dockside pubs and night-spots. He may not like the local beer, nor may he enjoy the evening's activities, but he nevertheless goes along with his fellows simply to gain their acceptance.

This need for acceptance leads us on to the very root of group behaviour and discipline.

However large an organization, it breaks down into prime groups of not more than ten or twelve workers—the organization, itself, remains the secondary group. An understanding of these prime groups is most important for it is through them that we can influence behaviour. In a ship, for example, the prime groups would be the deck officers, the engineer officers, the sailors, the firemen, and the stewards. The ship is the secondary group. Each man on board is a member of one prime group or another and he will only help and accept the aims of the secondary group (the ship) which coincide with the aims of his primary group. Take, for example, the rigging of the gangway on arrival in port. The ship needs the gangway out for customs officers, stevedores and others to get aboard. Standing on the quay may be the agent, clutching mail in one hand and money in his other. The sailors want that mail and money and they know that they cannot get it until the gangway is rigged. The gangway is rigged without delay, for it satisfies the aim of the primary group. The ship (the secondary) also benefits for it, too, needs the gangway to be rigged. In this case, then, the aims of the primary coincide with the aims of the secondary and there is no difficulty in getting the job done. If, however, at 0300 the next morning the same sailors are told that, owing to a change in tide, the gangway is in danger of being damaged and needs to be shifted they will be loth to turn out to move the gangway and, from their bunks, will suggest what should be done with the gangway, the ship and the company! In this case the aims of the secondary (to have the gangway moved) do not coincide with the aims of the primary (to sleep) and indiscipline results.

If the aims of the secondary group clash with the aims of the primary, then no amount of propaganda or disciplinary threats will secure the wholehearted co-operation of the worker in furthering the aims of the secondary. The prime group has a code of behaviour which it forces on its individual members by threatening to ostracize anyone who breaks the code. This is often seen in the classroom where, for example, there may be a group of Second Mates studying for their certificates. In the same class may be one man who is forever asking questions, so much so that the rest of the group feel that this one man is retarding their progress. After a while, the members of the class will start sucking their teeth and muttering scornful remarks each time this one man asks a question. If this man is at all sensitive, he will stop asking questions for fear of further rejection, even though he may really want clarification of a certain point.

Each prime group has a natural leader who may or may not be the man holding the highest official rank. If the natural leader is also the official leader, then there are very few problems, but if the natural and official leaders are two separate men, there are bound to be problems and strife. In a ship where, for example, the Bosun is the strongest man on deck and the best seaman, there are no problems. But, on a ship where the Bosun is weak and ineffective and in the messroom is a tough hard, natural leader, problems are bound to arise. In the former ship the Chief Officer knows that any order he gives to the Bosun will be carried out by the crew, while in the latter ship the Chief Officer doubts whether his orders to the Bosun will be carried out by the whole deck crew. It is in this latter type of ship that we find the Bosun personally carrying out the less pleasant task while the rest of the crew only do the easier work. When this conflict between natural and official leaders arises on board a ship, one of the two should be removed. Quite often it pays to remove the weak, official leader and to promote the natural leader to official rank. Before making a decision on which of the two should be removed, the officers concerned must try to determine whether the removal of one "trouble-maker" will enable the official leader to exercise his authority properly (without the risk of the group throwing up another natural leader) or whether the promotion of the natural leader to official rank will cause disharmony due to wrong motivation on this man's part.

To sum up this second reason for work, we must restate that it is the job of management to see that, as far as is possible, the aims of the primary groups coincide with the aims of the whole organization. If any changes are to be made in undesirable behaviour, the initial step must be to discuss the matter with the group as a whole and finally, due regard must be paid to the natural leader of each group.

A third reason for work is for satisfaction. Whatever their jobs may be, many people like to feel that they have done their work well and have given to their jobs a little more than they need have done. The feeling of satisfaction and well-being is accentuated in the successful enterprise as each member of the group rightly feels that he contributed to its success. As far as possible we should try to generate a feeling of success in our ships and companies and to encourage all hands to add to the ship the little extras which will make her a smarter vessel. This feeling of enthusiasm must come from the top. If the managers and marine superintendents are despondent about the future, this despondency will be picked up by the officers and then, in turn, by the crew. It is in that sort of company where we find the dirty, badly painted ships with footmarks on the rails and "Irish pennants" hanging from the lifeboats. There is no feeling of pride in the ship. On the other hand, we find, in successful companies, that the ships are smart and well painted. There is an air of success throughout the ships and no-one would dare stand with his foot on the rails.

Most shipping companies employ public relations officers whose job is to see that the company's best image is kept before the public. Companies would find that a lot of good would come from this same image being put before the men in their ships. Instead of concentrating on circular letters to ships deploring wastage (as many companies appear to do), shipping management should concentrate on telling the men at sea just how successful a particular ship or voyage has been. This may, of course, present problems to the shipowner who could never report a successful voyage but, then it could be argued, he should not be in the shipping business.

Still pursuing the importance of satisfaction in work, it is worth spending a moment's thought on structural developments in ships. We notice that in many modern ships brasswork, teak rails and wooden decks have completely disappeared. This has been done, we are told, because in this age of high labour costs, a shipowner can no longer afford to keep these items clean. This is probably true, but careful thought needs to be given to the design of a ship and to the supply of the stores needed to keep her a smart ship instead of a rusty, floating, steel box. How many Chief Officers are there at sea today who feel frustrated simply because a shortage of paint and stores prevents them from smartening up their ships?

The fourth and last reason for work is for status. To some men, this may be the most important reason for choosing a particular job. Everyone needs to feel that he has a well-defined status and function. However grand or lowly his job, he needs to feel that it is benefiting society.

There are two types of status—intrinsic and derived—but, before examining these in depth we should examine status as a whole and ask if, in Britain, seamen enjoy the status they deserve. Because of the closed dock system which operates in Britain, members of the public rarely see seamen at work on their ships;

they only see them ashore at play. In South African, Australian and New Zealand ports, and in the ports of some other countries, members of the public have free access to the docks; they see the ships at work and the seamen derive a great deal of pleasure in showing landsmen around their ships. In those countries, seamen are fairly well integrated with society ashore; they enjoy a certain amount of status. In Britain, however, this is denied them and, in fact, ships' personnel in many companies have to go through a degrading and embarrassing procedure to obtain passes for friends to visit their ships. The most careful thought needs to be given to overcoming police, customs and dock authority objections in order to open the docks of Britain to the public. Possibly the greatest beneficiaries would be British shipowners, for if members of the public could see the fine conditions in many modern ships, there would probably be an increase in the number of men applying to go to sea.

We must, however, get back to our close examination of derived and intrinsic status. The former is simply derived from the position a man holds and has nothing to do with his personal attributes, while the latter is personal and depends entirely on the man's skill, abilities and qualities. This intrinsic status is by far the better of the two. Intrinsic status leaves room for all—the best lawyer in a town is not the less respected because someone else is the best doctor. So, if a cook on board a ship is the best cook in the fleet, he will enjoy respect and intrinsic status even though he does not hold the highest official rank on board.

People are striving for status all the time. They should be striving for intrinsic status by perfecting their skill and craftsmanship, but judging by the number of modern titles given to workers ashore many are striving for derived status.

Derived status comes from the position a man holds. It may give him power over others or it may simply give him a particular title. The Master and each officer in a ship has derived status which comes from the rank he holds and not from his personal qualities. The successful leader is one who enjoys both intrinsic and derived status. A man may be respected because he is Master of the ship but he is respected far more if he is the "best" Master in the fleet.

Derived status has its uses. A ships' officer is given a rank, a uniform, and gold braid on his arm in order to help him project the image of an "order giver". This is best illustrated by taking an example ashore. Let us imagine that we were standing on a pavement in London and saw approaching us, a well-dressed man complete with bowler, brief-case and rolled umbrella. We would probably think he was a manager or "order giver" in his firm. If, following a few yards behind, came a man scruffily dressed, with cloth cap and open-necked shirt, we would probably think he was an "order taker" in a firm. We could be completely wrong in our estimation, for the bowler hatted man may be a very junior clerk in an insurance company while the second man may be the foreman of a steel works and have lots of power. Yet our initial impression was that the first man was an order giver and the second an order taker. This illustrates one reason for officers being given uniforms; it is to help them in the order-giving situation.

A uniform must, of course, be properly worn if it is to project the image of "order giver". If we go back to the example used above, we can picture what an object of ridicule and amusement the neatly dressed man would have been if, instead of black shoes he had worn veldschoens and if the crown of his bowler had been pushed inwards. The same applies to uniforms for, if an officer were to wear brown shoes or a coloured shirt with his uniform jacket and trousers, he too would become an object of ridicule.

While on the subject of uniforms, we should consider the importance of consistency. In all aspects of human relations, and this includes the wearing of uniforms, consistency is always the key to success. If we are to wear a uniform we must either wear it properly all the time or not wear it at all.

There are, of course, many times when an officer needs to wear a boiler suit—when working in the engine room, when inspecting tanks, and when working on the heavy lift derrick are examples of some of these occasions. What we must guard against is wearing nondescript clothes at sea and only putting on our uniforms for arrival in port or for official visitors to the ship. In fact nothing creates greater amusement among dockers and ratings than to see the officers getting dressed up for the daily visits of the Marine Superintendent; they look upon this occasional dressing up as pretentious sham. Ratings respect uniforms and like to see their officers properly dressed. A Second Officer, for example, who wears his uniform properly all the time will soon find that his team of ratings will suggest that he does not help with the ropes and stoppers while berthing even though he is prepared to do so.

It is essential that an officer never over-estimates his self-importance simply because of the rank he holds. No officer should think that he is infinitely superior to the ratings and that they should never question his orders or views. In many cases there is little difference between the intelligence of an officer and a rating and the social rank of the parents is not a factor to be disregarded when considering officers and ratings in the Merchant Service.

The slight difference between officers and ratings may be illustrated in the following way. Suppose a certain Army regiment needed tall recruits and suppose a hundred fit and suitable candidates came forward. Suppose that all these candidates were academically and physically acceptable but that there were only twenty vacancies in the regiment. It is probable that the tallest twenty would be chosen and the remaining eighty rejected. In the minds of all those men, twenty would be classed "tall" and eighty "short", even though the heights of all of them may have ranged over only 3 inches from, say, 5 feet $11\frac{1}{2}$ inches to 6 feet $2\frac{1}{2}$ inches. If, however, there had been fifty vacancies, the tallest fifty would have been chosen and the remaining fifty classed as being "short". Thirty men, therefore, would have been classed as being short or tall depending on the number of vacancies. The same applies, to large extent, to the selection of officers for the Merchant Service, and for all the other Services: as the need alters, so standards are raised or lowered. In many cases there is very little difference in the intelligence of some officers and some ratings, a point which is recognized by the brighter ratings. There are, of course, some men at the lower end of the intelligence scale who could never be officers, no matter how great the need, and there are others, at the opposite end of the intelligence scale, who would be wasted if they were to serve as ratings. We should, however, never fall into the error of imagining that all ratings are crowded together at the bottom of the intelligence scale and that all officers are crowded together at the very top; there is a great deal of overlapping around the middle of the scale.

The small difference between officers and ratings means that every man fortunate enough to fall on the officer side of the scale should continuously be engaged in trying to improve himself. The importance of this statement cannot be over-emphasized. An officer should strive at all times to improve himself, for the most potent tool in leadership is personal example. If an officer sets a good example, his management of men will be made all the easier. If he has integrity, humility and humour, others will follow him. An officer should try to increase his feeling for the importance of the work in which he is engaged and then his subordinates will become more enthusiastic for the job. The Master of a ship, and every officer for that matter, must be a model to those below for, while a worker or rating may excuse certain weaknesses in his fellow-workers, he disapproves of them in his superiors. Untruthfulness, broken promises, forgotten regulations, drunkenness and sloppiness all help to destroy a rating's loyalty towards an officer. If a rating is to subordinate himself to an officer, he must really believe that that officer is his superior.

All officers, and ratings for that matter, should be striving for intrinsic status yet, in ships as they are today, the importance of derived status is somewhat over-stressed. We are apt to think of the Master as being the most important man on board and then, in order of importance, the Deck, Engineer or Catering Officers (depending on our personal viewpoint!), the sailors, the firemen and the stewards, with the deck and galleyboys being at the bottom of the importance scale. This outlook is wrong for two very good reasons. Firstly, the Master would be just as ineffectual without a crew as the crew would be without a Master. Secondly, no-one, not even the Master, is irreplaceable. The Chief Officer could take command if the Master were lost or left the ship. The Second Engineer could take over as Chief Engineer and one of the sailors could be promoted to Bosun if this were necessary. So let us not look down on another man as having a job simpler or less important than our own. Everyone on board contributes in one way or another to the successful prosecution of the voyage and to the welfare of everyone else on board.

In a ship, as in factories ashore, only part of a man is needed to perform a particular job. In many cases we are apt to look on that necessary part as being the whole man—an outlook which can cause a great deal of harm. Every worker, and that includes every officer and every rating, is, primarily, a whole, complete individual and, secondly, a workman. Each man on board a ship is working for the same reasons as every other man and his psychological needs are the same as the others' needs.

The average man needs social status in his workshop, office, street or ship. Lack of status makes some men strive all the harder for it while the same lack depresses others. Whenever possible, social status should be given to others for, as was once said, "Every man is my superior in that I may learn of him." We should try to give every man his due.

This leads straight on to self-respect. The man who loses his self-respect is never a very happy person, yet it is very easy to lose self-respect in this welfare state of ours. There are pension funds, education grants, unemployment benefits and free medical services and, if we are left with any worries, we can get an insurance company to take them from us on the payment of an annual premium!

The more that is done for people the more dependent they become on the system providing the benefits. They conform more and more to the accepted pattern. Once people start following the crowd they stop taking chances and their initiative dies. Dependency shows an incomplete personality. Let us, therefore, guard against increasing this dependency.

A man should not accept too much from the firm for which he works. Some companies offer pensions, sick-benefit schemes, house purchase plans, educational loans for employees' children, sports facilities, and a host of other fringe benefits. Some of these offers are very good and are worth accepting, but before taking advantage of these benefits a man should make sure that he will still be contributing towards his own welfare and towards the welfare of his family. He should make sure that he does not become too dependent on these fringe benefits for then he will become a "company's man"; he will become moulded into the type of person the company requires and will not be able to afford to leave that company; he will stop taking chances and will suppress his initiative for fear of losing his job. Such is not a very happy man.

A man is helped to keep his self-respect by his superior taking an interest in him. Every man likes to be appreciated, firstly as a person and secondly as a good workman. Mere verbal praise, empty of sincerity, does not give a man an inward glow of satisfaction. Much better than an off-handed "well done" is a short chat between the officer and the rating. The officer may ill afford the time, but a short chat does much to bring out the wholeness of a man. It is not suggested here that the Master should walk around the ship having lengthy yarns with everyone on board, but, whenever possible, he should try to have a few words with his junior officers and ratings.

Individual responsibility leads to self-respect and inward satisfaction. There are some jobs where there is very little scope for individual responsibility, but there are many jobs where a man is denied the inward satisfaction which comes from being responsible for a particular operation by the obsessional condition of his superior—that is, the superior feels that only he is competent to deal with every little detail.

Take, for example, a young officer on watch at night. If an alteration of course is to be made during his watch, and if he has clear instructions to alter course to a certain position, he will probably watch the position of the ship very closely and, at the right instant, make the required alteration of course. He derives some inward satisfaction from being trusted to carry out this operation and his mental faculties are sharpened. On the other hand, if his instructions were to not alter course but to call the Master beforehand so that he—the Master—could make the alteration, then this young officer would get no satisfaction out of the operation and his lack of interest would probably mean that his mental faculties would be dulled and his position fixing would be only approximate.

It is most important that Masters and senior officers on board ship delegate work to their experienced juniors whenever possible. Delegation of work is a habit which can be cultivated during an officer's earlier years. As a Third Officer, for example, he can delegate certain tasks to the cadets; as Second Officer he can delegate tasks to cadets and ratings; when he becomes a Chief Officer he can delegate work to cadets, ratings and the junior officers. Having formed this habit, he will then be more likely to delegate work to others when he is promoted to Master—and this will make for a happy ship.

Self-respect comes from a man knowing himself. A man must get to know himself if he is to be a good leader, but he will not get this understanding by simply answering the questions in a popular paper-back book on *How to Psycho-analyse Yourself*. He will only get to know himself if he answers honestly the following four questions:

    (1) What am I doing?
    (2) Why am I doing it?
    (3) Where am I going?
    (4) How am I going to get there?

A young officer may answer (1) by saying that he is going to sea and (2) by saying that he likes going on leave with more money than his contemporaries ashore. Question (3) is the most important of the lot. A young officer, or any other man for that matter, must decide where he wants to be when he is 50, and where he wants to be at 40 (the two goals must, of course, be related). If, at 50, he wants to be Marine Superintendent of a shipping company, then question (4) is easily answered; he will need to get the highest qualifications open to him. If, on the other hand, he decides that, at 50, he would like to be managing director of a sweet factory, then question (4) is best answered by his marrying the chairman's daughter or by getting into the sweet business without delay.

All of us must answer the four questions very seriously for when we go to work (whether at sea or ashore) we sell part of ourselves. We sell our mental and physical effort and our freedom to go where we like when we like. We must decide, in the light of our answers to the questions above, whether the price we are paid is enough; and price, here, does not only mean wages, but includes the security, status and satisfaction which every man needs to get from his job.

CHAPTER 2

Human Relations

THERE are some people in industry who believe that any improvement in human relations will make their employees work harder and produce more. There are others, at the opposite end of the employment scale, who believe that any improvement in human relations is a trick on "their" part (the bosses) to get more out of "us" (the workers). Neither outlook is correct for good, sound, human relations must be based on the golden rule of doing unto others what you would have them do to you.

Are human relations in the Merchant Navy as good as they might be? Are seamen frustrated? Is there excessive criticism of management by the men in the ships and vice-versa? Is indiscipline rife and is the turnover of labour too high? Do many shipmasters and officers at sea today feel unable to manage their crews properly?

If the answers to any of those questions are in the affirmative then we need to examine individual and group behaviour in the shipping industry for every pattern of behaviour has a cause. Only when the cause is recognized can the behaviour be understood. If the behaviour of any group in the industry is undesirable then the remedy lies in altering the human factors affecting the group. This, in turn, means that we shall need to pay more attention to human factors and less to wages and material comforts.

A working group, such as the crew of a ship, consists of a number of men each with his own personality and peculiarities. We cannot, therefore, explain away undesirable behaviour of the whole group by suggesting that each member of the group suffers from the same weaknesses or abnormalities; and yet this is so often done by managers and others when discussing inefficiency or indiscipline among their workers. We hear phrases like "*All* young people are hopelessly irresponsible" or "*All* crew members are indisciplined troublemakers". Quite often the behaviour of the group is compared with the behaviour of similar groups in the past, or with the way the observer thinks he behaved in the past. We hear phrases like "Young people used to take an interest in their jobs" or "There was never this sort of trouble with crews before the war". The use of these phrases shows a false—indeed, a dangerous—attitude of mind for the observer begins to believe that he is superior to the group he is discussing and he ignores the part he has played in bringing about this undesirable group behaviour. It also shows that he has not fully grasped the factors affecting a modern working group.

This sort of attitude can sometimes be observed among marine superintendents and managers of shipping companies who regard the behaviour of crews with a combination of irritation, helplessness and superiority. What is often overlooked is that it is the ship manager who has the power to create the right atmosphere in his ships. Members of the crew do not have this same power. It is no use managers saying "The more we give our crews, the more they ask for" or "The more we do, the less they do". This simply indicates that management is giving or doing the wrong things.

Conditions at sea today are nothing like those of thirty or forty years ago. In those days crews would not have dreamt of asking for swimming pools and ice-cream. Since the war, however, material conditions at sea have been made closer and closer to those obtaining ashore so, asks the sailor, why not make working conditions at sea exactly the same as those ashore? As long as ship managers think only of material comforts and ignore the self-respect and psychological needs of sailors they will go on giving additional material comforts and the sailors will continue to ask for more. Sailors do not need cinemas and tiled swimming pools as much as they need to be treated as whole, complete persons. This over-emphasis on the material things of life while ignoring the human factors shows incompetence on the part of management.

Some of the more enlightened shipping companies have already realized the importance of good human relations at sea and have brought their sea staff more into their confidence. Many more companies will need to alter their attitudes to their seamen if they are to keep their competitive positions in this changing world. As was mentioned in the first chapter of this book, all of us need to feel that we "belong" to one group or another and we need to know what is going on.

A research project carried out between 1960 and 1965 showed that one of the main causes of discontent and labour turn-over at sea is frustration. This point was confirmed later in a book *Managers and Men*†[16] in which the author stated that frustration is the biggest bar to progress in merchant ships; that the men at sea do not really understand what is happening on the shore side of their shipping companies and are so incensed by the apparent wastage ashore that they decline to take any positive steps to reduce wastage of time and stores on their own ships.

Frustration occurs when there is a gap between what a man has and what he feels he is entitled to and discontent increases the more a person feels his goal is attainable. People are more likely to be frustrated by the interference of another person or persons than by the material conditions under which they are working. For example, the officer of a ship, whose early training has led him to believe that he would have responsibilities once he became a qualified ships' officer, would feel far more frustrated by his Captain treating him as an irresponsible young man than he would by the monotony of the voyages or by the speedy turn-rounds in port. A Chief Officer who has pride in his ship and who has the desire to demonstrate his ability to keep a smart ship feels frustrated when his immediate superior ashore refuses to give him any more paint. The crew of a ship feel frustrated if they believe that any legitimate complaints they may have are blocked by the Master and are never passed on to the management of the company.

Frustration leads to poor human relations in a group and the

†Superscript numbers refer to the Bibliography at the end of the book.

symptoms are very easy to detect. There is an unusual amount of malicious gossip, suspicion, quarrelling, and sluggish work—the whole group appears to be working at its limit yet is not working very efficiently. One can feel the unrest and apathy in the group. Communications are poor and there is resentment of anything new. Equipment and stores are wasted or destroyed. There is antagonism towards superiors and, when human relations are very bad, there is a great deal of friction between the workers themselves. Needless to say, all this leads to a high labour turnover.

There is no need for human relations to remain poor but it calls for effort on the part of management, executives and officers to improve the working climate.

In this acquisitive society of ours far too much importance is attached to material gains yet, surely, the amassing of wealth should not be our true aim in life? The goal of society should be human happiness and satisfaction, and this goal cannot be reached until men are happy at their work. This is where human relations come in for good human relations make people happier in their work and encourage them to give of their best. It tries to achieve this by making round pegs fit into round holes and by making the conditions under which a man must work more acceptable to him and his family.

Happiness breeds efficiency and reduces labour turnover for there is no denying that when men are happy at work they produce more and their work is of a higher standard than when they hate the work on which they are engaged. The whole of society benefits from this, not only the shareholders of the company employing these men. Every individual and group in industry has a duty to society to be as efficient as possible and to treat other people as human beings. We cannot achieve this correct state of affairs unless everyone is emotionally healthy, and emotional health arises from an appreciation of workers as persons and not merely as economic units.

Working must be more than simply earning a living for, through work, we should be able to earn self-respect and the respect of our fellows. Work that is sheer drudgery is not worthy of men. In industry, good human relations takes into account each individual's needs and desires and helps him to keep his self-respect. Each man has his own views on politics, religion, and on the distribution of wealth yet all of us must work together and, at sea, we must live together. Conditions should be such that each man is free to think as he likes and is not forced to subject his beliefs to the will of those about him.

Take, for example, a young Third Officer on the bridge at night. He may be a strong supporter of one political party. The Master, a strong supporter of the other political party, may come out on the bridge to check on the weather and ship's position before turning in. As usually happens, he may have a few minutes' chat with the Third Officer. The Third Officer may happen to mention something in favour of his party. The Master may pick up this point, refute it, and, in a domineering manner, tell the young Third Officer that one political party is completely right and the other completely wrong. Because of the difference in rank between the two men, the Third Officer will not be able to come out with anything more than a few "Yes Sir's". The Master will then stalk off the bridge believing that he has put his young officer on the right political lines when all he has done, in fact, is to fill the Third Officer with resentment.

In these days of take-over bids and huge, impersonal corporations, people are finding themselves absorbed into larger and larger organizations and, unless they are close to the top, they no longer meet the owners, directors or managers of the firms for whom they work. They know little of the achievements, policy and future of their firms and soon lose their sense of loyalty. In all firms there must be of course, both givers and takers of orders. It is the job of management to see that order takers realize that they are important and necessary members of the organization.

Most people thrive in an atmosphere which enables them to be themselves, but we must not think that, by loosening all the reins of discipline and treating everyone in a kindly manner, all industrial ills will be healed. No two people are exactly alike and each needs to be treated differently. Some need to be treated firmly and like to be told exactly what to do and the order in which each step of the job should be done. Others need to be given a broad direction about the job to be done and then left alone to get on with it. As we mentioned at the beginning of this book, each manager needs to develop those techniques which best suit his personality and it is worth adding here that, in a particular situation, a manager needs to take into account the personality of the man with whom he is dealing and adjust his own technique accordingly. If exactly the same approach is used on each man it will soon be recognized as an insincere technique of management and will do more harm than good.

In order that the working climate in any organization may be improved, there must be emotional maturity in the management and officers. Management must be genuinely interested in the welfare of the workers and must ensure that departmental heads, masters and officers carry out their duties in this field. The most important requirement is sincere interest at management level, for excessive bull and propaganda is soon recognized as a company's lack of faith in its ideas or as a man's lack of faith in his own ideas or competence. The differences between various shipping companies, so far as sincerity of interest in their men is concerned, is quite striking. Some companies have fitted all available amenities in their ships and yet the men do not look on those companies as being good companies .This is simply because of lack of genuine interest on the part of management. In some other companies, however, where because of the age of the ships the amenities on board are not quite up to modern standards, the men are happy simply because they can feel the sincere interest management takes in their well-being; they feel that they "belong".

In a firm where human relations are good, there is a feeling of pride and loyalty. There is no excessive inter-departmental rivalry and the manager of each section knows what is going on in the other departments. The simplest way of detecting good human relations is to observe workers when in the presence of anyone from authority. They carry on with their work calmly and normally and, if a worker happens to be talking to a colleague when his boss arrives on the scene, he will complete his conversation in a normal, human manner. When human relations are poor, such is not the case for, on the arrival of the boss, the workers either become abnormally active or they glower at the boss until he speaks or leaves the room. Nothing is more indicative of the poor human relations in the Merchant Service than the subservient attitude adopted by some Masters and officers when in the presence of anyone from "the office".

Take, for example, the way dozens of shore officials, agents and clerks all barge into the Master's room in port and are welcomed by the Master. Yet, if the Master wanted to see any one of those officials ashore he would have to knock on the official's door and then wait until that official was ready to admit him.

Another good example of this occurred when a ship berthed at 0900 one morning. The Chief Officer had not had his breakfast (why do ships always seem to berth at meal-times?) and the steward was waiting for him. Also waiting to see the Chief Officer was a clerk from the office. This clerk had had his breakfast and was quite prepared to wait for the Chief Officer. Suddenly the Master interfered and ordered the Chief Officer to delay his breakfast until he had dealt with this clerk. The Master felt that he was doing his duty to the Company; the Chief Officer felt resentful; and the clerk felt that he must be a very important man to be given this special treatment. On receiving similar treatment from all the ships he visited, this young clerk soon became so inflated with self-importance that he came to expect special treatment from ships' officers. On the rare occasions when he was treated firmly and fairly on a particular ship, he would go back to the office with stories of rudeness.

One step to be taken in improving the working climate at sea is to show the ships' officer just where he fits into the organization. He will thus have greater confidence in dealing with shore officials firmly and fairly instead of treating every man from "the office" as his superior. Good communications lie at the root of improving the working climate at sea and this important subject is dealt with in the next chapter.

Let us now look at human relations from a more personal point of view.

When a man does not understand himself he is unable to control his emotions and is easily led by politicians, salesmen, editors and others. A man should try to get to know himself, not, as was mentioned earlier in this book, by getting a "Do it Yourself" book on psycho-analysis, but by answering the four questions: What am I doing, why am I doing it, where am I going, and how am I going to get there? A man *must* have a purpose and then he can work efficiently towards it. If he has no goal he tends to look on all the daily irritations and indisciplines as blocks to his progress towards he knows not where.

An efficient man is proud of his own and his company's progress. He knows how to do his job and why it needs to be done. He gives to his job a little more than he needs give. He listens to other points of view and changes his own programme when a better one is suggested. Most important of all, he is self-disciplined and self-discipline in people is industry's greatest need. Often people talk of their rights and yet rarely are they fully aware of their responsibilities to their work.

It is not enough for a man to be an expert in one field of technology; he must also take other people into account. Ashore, much of our day and, at sea, all of our day is spent with other people. We should try to be reasonable and see other people's points of view. We should be tolerant and sensitive to atmosphere and we should never try to impress others with our own importance.

When we look around us we usually find that the men we like and respect most are those who are courteous to all around them —their superiors, equals, and juniors—for uncouthness and foul language earn nothing but dislike.

Everyone, whether he be a manager, officer or rating needs to be liked. This need frequently sets a problem for the manager or officer who finds himself torn between duty to his company and sympathy for his subordinate when this man has committed some act of indiscipline. If ever this happens, the golden rule is: never exchange your control of the situation for the affectionate regard of your subordinates. For example, the Master faced with a rating who has disobeyed an order and who should be punished may think that if he does not punish the rating, the rating will like him. The instant the Master does this, he has lost for he has sold his control of that rating and will have the greatest difficulty in getting control back again. The reason for this is that, in many face to face situations, one person tries to dominate the other. The rating, in the situation described above would dearly love to control the Master and he achieves this the instant the Master lets him off. It is not suggested that harsh punishment should be meted out to a man whenever he breaks a regulation or disobeys an order, for all the circumstances of the case must be taken into account. Nevertheless, it is safer to be too strict than too soft.

Another human problem facing industry today is that of helping young people and new-comers find their right place. The pace of industry is changing so rapidly that recruits are often left confused and do not have a clear understanding of what is expected of them. The result is that they do what they think they should, and this may or may not be the correct thing. It is up to managers or senior officers to tell new-comers what they should do; the new-comer should not have to ask.

Take, for example, a Second Officer who returned to a new ship after his leave. On his last ship the Master laid off all the courses on the charts and all this Second Officer was required to do was to clean off the charts and get them placed in their correct sequence. Thinking that this was the right thing to do (in the ship he had just joined) the Second Officer simply got out the new charts and put them in the right order. It came time for sailing. The Master went up on the bridge, took out the first chart (expecting to find the courses laid off) and found that the chart was bare. He called up the Second Officer and reprimanded him for not laying off the courses. The Second Officer's reply was that he did not think that he had to. The Master did not accept this excuse for, he said, *all* Second Officers lay off courses. The

Second Officer then, filled with resentment, had to get down to laying off all the courses. The fault, in this example, laid with the Master for he should have told this officer exactly what he wanted done and should not have left the officer to do what he (the Second Officer) thought he should do.

Whenever a new-comer joins a ship or group he should be told exactly what is expected of him. People respond to a kindly welcome and this should be more constructive than simply offering the new-comer a glass of gin.

Senior men should hand on all they have learned to those who follow. This is rarely done at sea today yet would be beneficial to all. Why do not more Masters teach their Chief Officers all they know about ship-handling and ship's business instead of leaving these officers on the focs'le head when entering port? Why do not more Chief Engineers teach their juniors the tricks of their trade? One of the most important duties of an officer is to train the fellow below him to take his job.

Training and education are dealt with later in this book but it is worth emphasizing here that each officer has a major role to play in the training of juniors whether they be junior officers, cadets or ratings. Training is a continuous process and no officer can train his juniors effectively unless he really gets to know them —and he can only get to know them by *talking* to them. The social gathering in a cabin for a drink before meals is not the best time to get to know juniors for then "shop" is often taboo. The best time to get to know people is at meal times. Senior officers should sit with their junior officers and cadets during meals. It is at these times that personal experiences, shipwork and the future commitments of the ship can be discussed in perfect freedom. The juniors cannot fail to learn from their seniors and, in turn, the seniors can learn what the juniors are thinking. Most important of all, the juniors will learn that there is an important difference between friendliness and familiarity and junior officers, learning this important fact of life by example in the saloon, can later apply it to their dealings with the crew.

One of the worst aspects of officer life aboard merchant ships is the rigidity of seating in the saloon with the Master, Chief Engineer and Chief Officer sitting at one table and the cadets banned to the furthest corner of the saloon or, worse still, made to eat in a separate room altogether. The Master may feel it wise to keep his one seat for status reasons, but there is no reason why he should not, on occasions, invite junior officers and cadets to sit with him. The other officers should be encouraged to mix freely at the saloon tables in order to build up a team spirit on board and to improve human relations. This is such a simple step to take: Why is it not taken?

To complete this personal aspect of human relations we should briefly consider power politics. In any group of people, whether they be employees in the same factory or members of the same voluntary organization, there are always some men trying to get ahead of their fellows. This is quite normal. If a man does not strive to get ahead he will be left behind, but, in so striving, a man should not sell his soul and scruples to get to the top.

In a ship, where ranks are clearly defined on the Articles at the start of the voyage, power politics are hardly necessary yet there are still some people trying to "get in" with the Master, Chief Engineer or Chief Steward. They are always around when a job needs to be done even though it should rightly be done by someone else. A power politician usually has a façade of friendliness to all, yet drops this and stops talking to his juniors the moment his superior arrives on the scene. Have we not all known the Chief Officer who, while talking to a group of other officers, will suddenly move away in order to catch the eye of the Master whose footsteps have just been heard on the deck above? These types of men attach importance to the wrong things and usually get worked up over real and imagined slights to their authority. These are the types who are weak disciplinarians when their boss is away, but who speak harshly to the ratings when in the hearing of the Master. We should not worry about these people, but should recognize them for what they are. A man should be continuously trying to improve himself in order to gain intrinsic status for it is much better to have power with people than over them.

CHAPTER 3

Communications

THE importance of good communications cannot be over-emphasized.

When communications are good all employees know what is going on; they have a broad understanding of the past achievements and future policy of their company and they have a clear idea of what is expected of them. They feel loyal towards their company. On the other hand, when communications are poor or non-existent workers do not know what is going on, they find no reason to identify themselves with the company and they probably sink their loyalty into some other organization.

Not only are communications important for the well-being of the workers, but they are also essential for effective management. Before coming to a decision, a manager must have a sound grasp of the wholeness of the issue for many a scheme has failed simply because all the relevant facts were not fully considered beforehand. A manager or shipmaster must, of course, delegate responsibility and work to others but he should do this in such a way that he will be kept fully informed of all that is going on. Communications must move vertically upwards as well as downwards. It is not enough for a manager simply to tell his men what they must do; he needs to know what his men feel about the proposed task or project.

The problems of communication are probably more difficult in shipping than in any other industry. Firstly, there is the barrier caused by the geographical separation of units of the shipping company spread all over the world. Secondly, there is the barrier caused by strongly graded ranks aboard ship.

The more severe of these two barriers is the gap that exists between head office and the ships. The fact of the matter, however unpalatable it may be, is that, in most companies, the sea staff simply do not know what is going on. They know what their jobs are and they know what is expected of them but they only have the vaguest ideas of the past achievements and future policy of their shipping companies. The only communications most of them receive from their head offices are books of instructions or condemnatory circular letters, most of which seem to start with the phrase "We fail to understand why . . . ".

Who is to blame for the poor communications between ship and shore? Surely it is the management of shipping companies who have failed to keep their sea staff fully informed on future trends. The sea staff cannot ask for information if they do not know what path their company is following. One of the most positive steps which can be taken to improve morale at sea is for all ship managers to make it their duty to keep their sea staff fully informed of all matters affecting the company. Ship managers should also ensure that they ask, positively, for a feed back of information from their ships.

We should not over-criticize shipping companies for their poor communications for there are many industries ashore where gaps exist between two sets of workers in one company. In a factory, for example, a communication gap often exists between the office staff and the workers on the shop floor. The clerks, being close to the management, know what is going on; they feel that they are part of the company and are loyal to it. The shop floor workers, being further removed from the management, do not always know what is going on; they do not identify themselves with the company and, quite often, sink their loyalty into an organization which does make them feel they "belong"— their trade union. We must not decry trade unions for they have an important part to play in achieving industrial harmony and each one of us has the right to associate with whom we choose. But, if managers want to combat the power of trade unions, they must keep their workers fully informed on all that is going on in their company.

The difference between office and shop floor workers in a factory is also found between shore clerks and ships' officers in a shipping company. The clerk usually knows what is going on in the company while the ships' officer does not. Quite often a discussion between shore clerk and ships' officer ends with the officer storming off saying to himself "That clerk thinks he *is* the company," when all the clerk did was to mention some fact about the future of which the ships' officer knew nothing.

Do seamen *really* know where they fit into their shipping company? In most cases the answer is in the negative, but this does not mean that nothing can be done to improve the situation. There are a number of methods which can be adopted to improve communications between ship and shore, and by far the most effective is to send sea staff to work in the company's office ashore.

If a shipowner were asked to define the whole purpose of his company he would rightly say that it was to make a profit. He would also be correct in pointing out that he needs specialized departments and specialized staff to run his organization efficiently. Of course, the heads of departments need to be experienced specialists but a great deal of the general work could be done more efficiently by men with a broader understanding of the whole organization than that held by men who had specialized too early in their lives.

There seem to be few reasons why all recruits to a shipping company should not go to sea to start with or, for that matter, why they should not all start off in the office together. In fact it would do some seamen a lot of good to see the pressure and conditions under which some office staff have to work; it may make them more contented at sea. The main purpose, however, in having a joint introduction to shipping is to bridge the gulf between ship and shore staffs of a shipping company.

During an investigation carried out among the shore and sea staffs of a particular company to determine how they saw each other, one officer described his company as a mighty pyramid. Sticking out of this pyramid was a long arm at the end of which happened to be some ships, and he happened to work on one of them. His view is illustrated in Fig. 3.1.

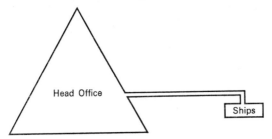

Fig. 3.1. The view of a shipping company through the eyes of a ship's officer.

The shore clerk, however, had a different view, as shown in Fig. 3.2. He saw a minute head office supporting a huge fleet of ships and, it is worth mentioning, his view was somewhat coloured by the very high wages and long leaves he felt were given to the sea staff.

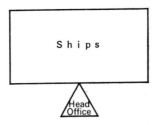

Fig. 3.2. The view of a shipping company through the eyes of a shore clerk.

The correct view of a shipping company, however, is illustrated in Fig. 3.3 and should be of the cargo traffic, passenger traffic, operations, finance, claims, stores, research and public relations departments all growing upwards together with the departmental heads collaborating to ensure the smooth and efficient running of the company. If this is the correct view, then thought can be given to the interchange of labour at equivalent grades for on close examination of a shipping company, it can be seen that there are a number of departments ashore in which ex-seagoing staff could be used effectively.

Even with his existing training and knowledge, a deck officer could be employed as a cargo booking clerk; possibly as a freight

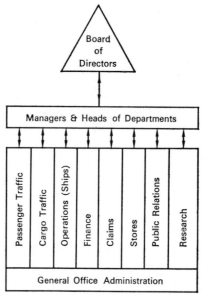

FIG. 3.3. The correct view of a shipping company.

canvasser; in all sections of the operations department, e.g. new buildings, repairs, appointments, training, ships' correspondence; in the claims department; in the stores department and in the research department. The engineer officer could be employed in all those sections of the operations department concerned with the technical aspects of ships; in the stores department; and in the research department. The Purser officer could be employed in the passenger department; in the finance department; in claims; in stores; and, finally, in the public relations department.

There may be many objections to the interchange outlined above. It is said that it takes many years for a shore clerk to learn the company's procedure and to build up the numerous contacts outside the company with whom he has to deal. It is also said that ships' officers would not take kindly to large reductions in their wages while working ashore in the office—shipowners could not be expected to pay seagoing rates of pay to all their office staff. It may also be argued that the highly competitive nature of the shipping industry calls for specialization and that a man could not be both an efficient ships' officer and an efficient shore clerk. All these objections may be sound and may prevent complete interchange of sea and shore staffs, but nevertheless, it is highly desirable to use as many seamen as possible in the company's office in order to bridge the gulf between the two sets of personnel.

Some companies are already using a number of their seagoing officers in their offices ashore, but their methods of selection differ. In one particular company, all the officers have been asked to state their preferences so far as sea and shore employment are concerned and their wishes are taken into account, as far as possible, when placing these men. In another company, all vacancies for positions ashore are advertised in the company's magazine and applications are invited from any sea staff who care to apply. Each system has its merits and one or the other should be used. Quite the worst way of selecting a man for effective work ashore is to pick, at random, any officer who happens to be on leave when the vacancy arises.

Another effective way of bridging the gulf between sea and shore staff, and of giving the sea staff an insight into the workings of the company, is by means of company conferences or short courses. Many companies are running these internal courses and, generally, these fall into three types.

The first is the one- or two-week course attended by sea-going officers only. This has the merit of enabling the company to arrange a series of lectures some of which are delivered by the company's own managers and deal with company policy while others are delivered by outside specialist lecturers on subjects of a more general nature. The disadvantage of this type of conference is that, apart from the manager lecturers, the sea staff do not get to know many of the office staff.

The second type of conference is usually of three or four days' duration and is attended by equal numbers of sea and shore personnel. Lectures are given and discussions held on both the shipping and office aspects of the company's operations. The great advantage of this type of conference is that staff from all sections of the company get to know each other and they gain an insight into each other's problems.

The third type of conference is more like a one-day meeting. It has the advantage of enabling the management of the company to put over their problems and the future policy of the company to a broader cross-section of their sea staff than they can to the small number of senior officers who attend the conferences outlined in the two types above. On the other hand, the disadvantage of this type of conference is that various points of interest can only be covered very briefly. One day a month is set aside for this type of conference and all the officers on leave are invited to head office on that day. In the morning they meet the marine superintendents who deliver brief lectures on current developments in the fleet and then deal with any questions which may arise. The officers then lunch with these superintendents and with other office staff and then, in the afternoon, they meet a few of the general managers or directors of the company who deal with the long-term, future developments of the company. On returning to sea after their leaves these officers are able to spread the news of any new developments which had been mentioned at the previous monthly meeting.

All these conferences are good and help to improve morale at sea. One type or another should be used by every shipping company.

Many shipping companies publish their own monthly magazines, some of which are excellent. The purpose of these magazines and journals is to keep all employees fully informed on all that is going on in the company. One of the best magazines is the one published by a Scottish Shipping Company[2] for it contains articles written by the management on future developments in the Company as well as brief articles on the activities of each one of the ships in the fleet. In other companies, however, the magazine is little more than a social diary and is usually amply illustrated with photographs of parties held during the previous month. In one company, the shipping news is nothing more than brief details of marriages, births, examination results and new appointments contained on one sheet of paper.

The shipping company magazine has an important part to play in keeping men at sea in touch with each other and in touch with current developments in the company; every effort should be made to ensure the magazine achieves this purpose.

Before leaving company magazines, mention should be made of an informative little booklet[3], issued by a particular company to all new employees. A brief outline is given of the past achievements, current developments and future policy of the company. More important is the information it contains on the organization and the responsibilities of the various people in the office so that a mother or wife, worried about mail, allotments or even the whereabouts of her man can refer to the booklet to see just whom she should telephone for help or advice. This approach of bringing the relatives of sea staff more into the confidence of the company is something which could be copied, to advantage, by other shipping companies.

Another effective way of spreading information throughout their fleet is by means of circular letters and accident reports which have to be initialled by each officer after he has read them. Unfortunately this is a one way flow of information and methods by which this flow can be reversed are discussed later in this chapter.

No matter how the news of a new development comes to a ship, it is important that it be told to all hands without delay. In most cases, the communication is sent to the Master and it is then left to him to tell his officers and crew. It is difficult to understand the mental workings of the Master who secretes the orders and other information, leaving his officers to be informed by the catering department!

There are a number of ways in which news may be spread properly throughout the ship. News of departmental interest only should be given to the head of that department and he should be instructed to pass it on to his junior officers and ratings without delay. The Master should ensure that this is done properly and not via the galley radio. If the news is of general interest, it should be given to all the heads of departments at the same time unless the working of the ship makes this impracticable.

It is absolutely essential that news affecting the crew be given to them in the proper form and without delay. This may be done verbally via the petty officers and senior ratings or, better still, by a carefully worded notice pinned on the crew's notice board. We all know, from childhood games, how messages are distorted when they are passed by word of mouth. This means that, if a Master wants to ensure the crew get the proper meaning of a message, the Master or a senior officer should address the whole crew mustered together or should send the message to them in writing. Another way of keeping the crew informed of all that is going on is by means of the Joint Consultative Committee meeting described later in this chapter.

Communications have a bearing on welfare. For the most part, all members of a ship's company are just as interested in the ship's whereabouts as are the navigating officers and probably the most effective way of getting this information to the crew is by means of a chart showing the noon position, the day's run, and a brief note on any points of land which are to be passed during the following twenty-four hours. This has been done for many years on passenger ships and could well be extended to cargo ships.

As was mentioned earlier in this chapter, communications, to be really efficient, must move vertically upwards as well as downwards. The two most effective ways of achieving this are by meetings or by suggestion schemes.

In ships manned under the dual-purpose system, management

meetings are held at regular intervals. These meetings are attended by the Chief Officer, the Chief Engineer, the Second Engineer and the Chief Steward, and are chaired by the Master. There is no reason why a Senior Petty Officer should not be invited to attend some of these meetings. Whether a Petty Officer is present or not, the minutes of the meetings, together with the work plan decided upon, should be displayed on the crew's notice board. This will help to keep them in the picture. The advantage of having a Petty Officer at some of the meetings is that he can keep the officers informed on the crew's reactions to various problems or decisions.

Another way of establishing a two-way flow of communication is by means of a joint consultative meeting, but before describing this system it should be understood that no call is being made here for the ship to be run by a soviet.

Many factories ashore have joint consultative committee meetings at regular or irregular intervals. These meetings are attended by representatives of management, office staff, shop floor workers, transport staff, canteen staff, etc. At these meetings, management is able to tell the workers of current plans in the factory, for example that the factory is to stop making extinguisher cases and is to tool up for a large order for grease guns. At the same time, the workers are able to come up with ideas for improving efficiency or with their complaints. They may, for example, ask the management why a toilet window, broken for the previous three weeks, had not been repaired. These joint consultative meetings contribute towards good communications and give workers the feeling of "belonging" to the enterprise. Why should not similar meetings be held aboard ship?

The Master, Chief Officer, Chief Engineer, Chief Steward, Bosun, one sailor, one fireman, and one steward could meet together to air their views and discuss common problems. The guiding of such a committee would call for a lot of wisdom on the part of the Master, but it would do a tremendous amount of good, the crew would feel that an interest was being taken in them as people and that their views and opinions were respected. The ideal time for such a meeting would be soon after the ship leaves port. The Master could explain the future commitments of the vessel and any disciplinary problems which may have arisen while in that port could be discussed. At the same time the crew could give their side of the picture and could, possibly, draw the Master's attention to certain injustices they may have suffered in that port. They may, for example, have been cheated on taxi fares or on laundry charges. The meeting need not be devoted entirely to the settling of complaints for all those attending should be encouraged to discuss ways in which the operational efficiency of the ship may be improved. The meetings need not only be held when the ship leaves port but whenever the circumstances warrant it.

Joint consultative meetings, as described here, have an additional advantage for they may prove to be the best defence a Master could have against shop-stewards. A full chapter is devoted to liaison representatives later in this book, but it is worth mentioning, at this stage, that if a shop-steward is given the right to hold private interviews with the Master he could, when reporting back to the crew, undermine the Master's authority by colouring, altering or omitting certain things said at those private interviews. If, however, the representative was made to present his complaints to the Master before the Consultative Committee, the committee would act as a sounding board, temper displays of emotion and allow the Master to deal with the complaint in a wise manner. Furthermore, if later the representative were to report back to the crew and colour anything the Master said, he could be corrected by the other ratings present at the meeting. The main purpose of these meetings, however, is to bridge the gulf between officers and crew on *the officers' initiative*.

Another way of securing a two-way flow of information is by means of suggestion schemes. In some companies, suggestion schemes are non-existent, in others sea personnel are instructed to pass on any ideas to their Marine Superintendents (who are usually far too busy with their day-to-day routine to devote much time to assessing new ideas) and in other companies still a box is screwed to a bulkhead in all ships and the sea staff are asked to post their suggestions in these boxes. Suggestion boxes can work, but it is not unknown for some suggestions posted in these boxes to be nothing more than inquiries into the parental background of the Mate, Master or shipowner!

The suggestion schemes outlined above are too passive, and a more positive method needs to be adopted if the best ideas are to be obtained. In municipal corporations ashore, architectural competitions are held when a new major building is contemplated. The corporations concerned employ staffs of architects who are quite competent to design new buildings, but, in order to obtain the best ideas available, architects from all over the country are invited to submit their designs for the new building. There are no cash prizes, but the winner of such a competition is engaged as consultant for the new project.

Similar competitions could be held among the officers and ratings of a fleet when a new ship is contemplated. It would be too much to expect any one officer to design a complete ship, but sea staff could be asked for their ideas on the layout of certain parts of the ship or on the equipment which should be provided. There need be no cash prizes for the best ideas; the men concerned will derive enough satisfaction out of having their ideas adopted. A shipowner introducing this scheme will find it advantageous to ask, by name, a limited number of officers or ratings to submit their ideas for certain parts of a new ship. Even if some of the ideas are impracticable, the men concerned will derive a certain amount of pride out of being asked by name to carry out some original and creative work for their company. Objectors to this scheme may say that if ten men were asked to design the layout of a bridge, ten different schemes would be put forward. This may be so, but each scheme may have one good point and it will then be up to the naval architects to incorporate some or all these good ideas in the new ship.

Still pursuing the point of getting seamen to submit their ideas on improving the operational efficiency of ships, it is worth mentioning the scheme launched by the Plymouth School of

Navigation during 1966. This school, which is part of a large college with extensive facilities for examining, testing and developing practically any navigational, engineering, electronic, chemical or nuclear device, offered to give a confidential assessment on any new idea submitted by a seafarer or shipping company. Up to the time of writing, dozens of ideas have poured in. Some were ill conceived and were rejected, but many of the ideas submitted were good and, after assessment and development, the ideas have, at the request of the seamen concerned, been passed on to manufacturers of nautical equipment.

To return to the point of establishing a two-way communication system, we should examine the idea of encouraging Masters, officers and ratings to submit operational reports. Up until the end of the last century, shipowners kept in touch with their best sources of commercial information—their shipmasters —by making daily visits to their ships in port. With the growth of larger companies and large offices ashore, shipowners have tended to devote more time to their offices ashore and less time to keeping in touch with their Masters and sea staffs. In order to regain this contact, and in order to learn what is going on in ports abroad served by their ships, shipowners should invite Masters to submit reports on their observations made in ports abroad. Masters could, for example, report on cargoes lying in the sheds abroad, on new cargo-handling devices being built, on local maritime, labour or political problems, and on many other aspects which may enable the shipowner to make the correct decisions on the future trading of his vessels. All the officers should be encouraged to report on the equipment or methods of operation of ships berthed near by which made those other ships more efficient than the officers' own ships. Everyone should be encouraged to report on the effectiveness or ineffectiveness of the equipment fitted on their own ships and to make suggestions for the re-siting of existing equipment whereby the operational efficiency of their ships may be increased.

CHAPTER 4

Group Management

VESSELS must be run as efficiently as possible. This means that officers must not only know how to do their own jobs, they must also know how to get the best out of their men. It is not enough for an officer to be a good navigator, engineer, purser or steward, he must know how to manage men and how to win their trust.

There are many definitions of leadership. Lord Montgomery defines it as "the capacity and will to rally men to a common purpose and the character to inspire confidence". When we think of a leader, we think of a man rousing the emotions of a group of people in order to lead them through adversities to their goal. A ships' officer, however, does not want to rouse the emotions of his crew for the glory of the ship and the shipping company. All he wants to do is to get the crew to work together efficiently and to get them to live together happily, no matter how diverse their views, behaviour and morals may be. So let us drop the word leadership and talk of group management when dealing with people collectively and man management when dealing with one man in a face-to-face situation.

All of us would learn something by reading the biographies of the great military, political and industrial leaders, but we would not become good group managers simply by emulating such men. The leaders referred to lived and operated in situations quite different to those existing on board merchant ships. Nor will an officer become a good group leader by simply reading one of the popular paper backs on *How to be a good leader*. He will only become a good group manager if he has a genuine liking for the men around him and has the desire to help them. His guiding principles should be based on a recognition of the dignity of men.

There are many desirable qualities a good group manager should have. He should be a good judge of human nature and it is essential that he be self-disciplined. One psychologist lists fifty qualities which are required by a good leader. These range from understanding and determination to foresight and a pleasing manner. There are, however, four qualities which are of the greatest importance and any man wanting to be a good group manager should try to develop these qualities in himself.

(1) The most important quality in a manager is that he must have the capacity for decision. As was mentioned in the previous chapter, the manager must ensure that he is kept fully informed of all that is going on—he needs to have all the threads of the business in his hands—but, once he has considered all the material facts, the manager *must* make a decision and he must communicate his decision to the men below him.

(2) The manager must be consistent and, if possible, consistently humane. The manager must be firm and fair but, above all, he must be consistent. Inconsistency simply destroys faithfulness.

Most people try to please the man above them but if his moods are changeable, if on one day he wants a job done in a certain way and yet on the next day he wants it done in a different way, the men below simply do not know where they stand and their faithfulness is destroyed.

(3) The manager should be accessible to all. Officers and ratings are all individuals who, from time to time, may have personal problems on which they require help and advice. The Master or Staff Captain should be prepared to give this help whenever it is asked for. So far as is possible, the Master should be consistent in his dealings with others. It should be possible for a man to approach the Master with a personal request at any reasonable time without first having to consider what mood the Master may be in. Then, too, and this has a bearing on consistency, the Master should preserve the same distance from all. He should not remain aloof; on the contrary, he should join in the spirit of

common venture. He should not, for example, strike up a very strong friendship with one officer (who may come from the same home town) to the exclusion of the other officers. When such a strong friendship is struck up, the Master may, inadvertently, pass on information to this one officer with the result that the other officers will feel "left out of it".

(4) The manager should be a thinker. He should confront problems with intelligence rather than with hasty generalizations. Too great a readiness to generalize shows weak judgement and a poor grasp of the whole issue. Short-tempered, hasty judgements anger subordinates.

One of the best habits an officer should try to develop is the habit of *thinking* before coming out with an answer to any question, or before giving an order. There are occasions, of course, when there is very little time to think but, if an officer thinks for a few seconds, or a few minutes or, if possible, for a few hours, before saying anything, his order will probably be better than if he had simply blurted it out on the spur of the moment.

In contrast to the desirable qualities in managers, let us examine those qualities which prevent men from handling others successfully.

The manager, master or officer should not be unduly exacting, for people are human and require a considerate approach to their occasional mistakes. If, for example, a master is forever criticizing the work of his officers they will feel under excessive pressure and will not work efficiently or happily. The same applies to the crew. If the Mate is forever criticizing their work they, too, will feel under pressure and their resentment of this incessant criticism will cause to make them work less efficiently. There are many ways of doing a particular job and the duty of the man in charge is to decide upon the goal and then lay down the broad limits between which the men must work. He should then let the men work in their own way to achieve the desired goal.

A manager should not personally attend to every little detail for, when he does, he is wasting his own and his firm's time. The Master of a ship, for example, is appointed to co-ordinate the efforts of those below him to secure the smooth and efficient operation of the ship. Those Masters who insist on dealing with every little thing that crops up do not understand their real duty nor the harm they do to the self-respect and self-esteem of their officers.

A hasty, spiteful man will never be a good boss, for while the spite may be directed at others, those workers within hearing will detest the manager who voices such feelings. Take, for example, a Master on the bridge with the Third Officer. Walking along the fore-deck may be the Second Officer. If, now, the Master says to the Third Officer, "Look at that Second Mate, what a scruffy officer he is. I bet he is going to make a mess of whatever he is going to do," all the Third Officer can say is "Yes Sir," but deep down he will be wondering if, on the next occasion that he walks along the fore-deck while the Master is on the bridge with another officer, the Master may come out with equally derogatory remarks about him. Everyone is free to think what he likes about other men but he should not voice these opinions in the hearing of others.

An unstable, moody man who broods over real and imagined slights to his authority will never be a successful group manager until he conquers this instability. This point may be illustrated with an example of what actually happened on a particular ship. On this ship the Master always lunched at 1230. The ship was in London and, as usually happens, there were numerous shore officials and relatives of the officers on board. The stewards knew that there would be insufficient seating in the saloon and, so that some seats would be available for the Master and his wife at 1230, the stewards asked the rest of the officers and their wives to lunch at 1200. Every seat in the saloon was filled, including the Master's. Unfortunately, the Master decided to go ashore that afternoon and went down to the saloon at 1200. There were no vacant seats for him and his wife and an angry scene resulted. Not only did the Master express his anger at the time, but for the whole of the next voyage the Master kept on at his officers about their rudeness in occupying his seat. By the end of the voyage, the officers were heartily sickened by the whole affair and were not quite the happy, faithful men they might have been.

Officers should look on their rank objectively and should try to decide whether slights are aimed at them personally or simply at the stations they hold. A man should never think that, just because he holds officer rank, he is infinitely superior to the crew and that they should never question his orders or views.

This leads on to the effects of power. All the world's great thinkers agree that power ultimately corrupts. Power often demoralizes a person, for it makes him cease striving to improve himself. And, if a person is not improving his stature, he is probably on the decline. We sometimes see this effect of power in a ship where a Master, who has had just sufficient ability to reach command, gives a bad report on his bright, efficient Chief Officer for fear that this officer may eventually overtake the Master and become a marine superintendent over him. Officers should realize that much of their power comes from the rank they hold and not necessarily from their personal qualities.

We should now examine the needs of the members of the group and the type of man they would like their head to be.

(1) A worker's greatest need is to be calmed, not upset, by the presence of his boss. Most people work under some sort of strain and they want a leader who will approach them calmly. In many circumstances, this calls for the exercise of a great deal of self-control on the part of the manager, but it pays dividends. If the boss is excited and nervous, this nervous excitement is picked up by the members of the group and they all get emotionally worked up. This is when accidents happen.

Most seamen can probably recall coming alongside with a very nervous or excited Master or pilot on the bridge. The pilot rushes from one bridge wing to the other, banging into the telegraph and tripping over the wheel-house steps. Orders are screamed at the Chief Officer on the focs'le head and at the Second Officer on the poop. There is nervous excitement throughout the ship. This is the time when springs get jammed and when anchors are dropped into mooring boats.

Quite often such nervousness in a Master or officer stems not from fear of damaging the ship but from fear of what the other officers and ratings think about him. A man who *knows* that he can do his job competently becomes more secure in himself; he becomes a confident leader and does not get emotionally worked up. On the other hand, a man who worries excessively about what others think of him is usually the man who has no clear goal in life; he is the one who has not really answered the questions given at the end of Chapter 1.

The effect of nervous excitement being picked up by the members of the crew is illustrated by an incident which occurred on a tanker. The ship was fully loaded with aviation spirit and a fire started under the focs'le head. The Chief Officer, who had been in his cabin, came rushing out, tripped down all the ladders, grabbed a fire extinguisher and ran forward. The pumpman, who had learned from many fire drills that his station was aft at the pumproom, saw the Chief Officer dashing forward so he, too, picked up an extinguisher and ran after him. The Chief Officer entered the starboard door of the focs'le and the pumpman entered the port door. A few moments later, the Chief Officer came out wiping foam from his eyes; he had been sprayed by the pumpman!

(2) The Master and every officer must be a model to those below. Crew members, like all other workers, may excuse certain moral weaknesses in their fellows but never in the men who are put over them. As was mentioned earlier in this book, if a rating is to subordinate himself to an officer he must really believe that that officer is his superior. This is not to say that the officers must never relax and enjoy themselves but in this connection it is worth recalling that one definition of a naval officer is that he is a man who knows *when* he may dance on the wardroom table!

(3) A worker likes to be appreciated. Every man has the urge to assert his own importance and if he is not appreciated he becomes bitter. Unfortunately this sets up a chain reaction for once a man becomes bitter he becomes less liked and less appreciated and he then becomes even more bitter. A lot of bloody-mindedness on the part of ships' crews stems from the officers not

expressing appreciation for work well done. Expressing appreciation does not, necessarily, mean giving the crew an extra tot. There are various ways of expressing appreciation and one of the simplest ways is by telling the man concerned that he has done a good job.

(4) A crew member does not want hasty, ill-judged criticism. The human mind is extremely vulnerable and one hasty word or unfair criticism will sow a seed of hate in a man's mind. He will become over-sensitive to all future utterances from that officer and will find fault with, or scoff at, everything that officer tries to do in the future. This was brought out in a particular ship where the Master had wrongly reprimanded the Chief Officer for some incorrect stowage of cargo. From that moment on the Chief Officer hated the Master and tried to undermine his authority by laughing behind the Master's back and coming out with phrases like "I wonder what the old fool is up to now" in the hearing of junior officers.

(5) Every worker and every rating wants to be recognized as a whole, complete person. On board a ship the officers are all individuals with separate and distinct titles whereas a fireman, sailor, or steward is one of many holding the same rating. All need individuality and the least an officer can do is to learn and use each man's name.

Each man is a whole, complete being and yet we tend to recognize only that part of him which we use at work. Ashore, this problem is not so acute for, while a man may be the paint-shop foreman at work, he is "Dad" to his children at home and "Bill" to his friends at his pub. At sea, however, where everyone lives on the job, a man may be the Second Engineer at work and is also known as "The Second" at all social gatherings. In many ships the officers do not use christian names among themselves and fail to use surnames when speaking to their petty officers and ratings. As a result, they tend to identify that part of the man which is used at work as the whole man. All officers should try to use christian and surnames more than they do; we need to show others that we recognize them as whole persons.

I always remember one Master who made a point of wishing each man on board a happy birthday when that man's birthday came round. At first, the crew looked on him as being slightly odd when, for example, he went aft to wish the galley boy or a fireman a happy birthday. Later, however, when the crew understood this Master's sincerity, they came to appreciate what he was doing and each man looked forward to a brief chat with that Master on his birthday. This is not passed on to readers as a gimmick they themselves may try for each officer will have to build up his own personnel management techniques based on his own personality. The point being made is that each officer should recognize the wholeness and dignity of each man under him.

(6) A worker does not want aggressive domination for this reminds him of his inferior status and fills him with hatred. The old-fashioned "bucko" Mate who shouted at the crew and who was prepared to fight any man who questioned his orders certainly got the work done, but not happily. With such an officer, the crew would become nervous and frightened and would plan their vengeance for a time when the opportunity presented itself. Fortunately, the days of very harsh and hard discipline are over and, today, an officer can only win the trust and loyalty of his men by his own integrity and ability, that is to say, by his intrinsic status.

Supervision

Most workers do not like to be supervised for they feel that their reliability and efficiency are being questioned. Yet, if a job is worth doing it should be supervised—not necessarily by the top man but by someone in authority. The rank or rating of the supervisor should be related to the job in hand. Sailors resent the Chief Officer standing over them when they are engaged in normal routine work about the ship; they work more efficiently when the Bosun is the appointed supervisor of this routine work. When more important or unusual work is being done—such as using the heavy lift derrick—these same sailors expect the Chief

Officer to be out on deck supervising their work and they would resent his delegating the supervision of this type of work to the Bosun. If work is to be supervised, then the man in charge must make sure that he is supervising the work and its execution and not the people doing it. Take the example of a cadet painting a bulkhead. He may be painting perfectly well, but his dungarees may be rather dirty and it may be obvious that they have not been washed for some weeks. If now the Chief Officer comes on the scene and reprimands the cadet for the state of his clothes, this cadet will be filled with a mixture of resentment and anxiety and will not work as well. It is, of course, the Chief Officer's duty to see that the cadets are neatly dressed, but any reprimands about dress should be delivered at a suitable opportunity and not when the cadets are engaged on some particular job.

Supervision must be constructive. When the supervisor arrives on the scene, he should not come out with generalizations but should say exactly what is wrong. Take, for example, a group of sailors painting a deck house. If the Chief Officer comes up and says that they have made a mess of the whole job, the sailors will not know exactly what is wrong. Instead he should point to any holidays that have been left, or to the backs of pipes which have not been painted. He should then issue clear orders to rectify these faults. Also, the supervisor should not nag right through the job like a housewife when her husband is papering the hall, instead he should deal with a number or all of the faults at the same time.

Supervision must be consistent. No good is served by the Chief Officer standing over the crew all morning then sleeping in the afternoon while the crew are engaged on the same task. If this happens the crew will wonder why the Chief Officer bothered to supervise them in the morning; they will probably think that he did so in order to impress them with his importance or to impress the "Old Man" with his efficiency.

It need hardly be said that the supervisor should know *how* the job should be done yet this point is not always fully appreciated. So far as normal deck work is concerned, most officers know how the various jobs should be done but such is not always the case when it comes to the supervision of cargo handling and stowage. Unless an officer fully understands *all* the safety precautions which should be taken, and draws the dockers attention to *every* breach of these precautions, they will resent his supervision for they will soon realize that the officer in question does not really understand all aspects of the work in hand. They will feel that he is trying to impress them with his importance by picking on the one or two breaches of precautions about which he knows a little.

Now that the various problems have been described, we can examine a few practical rules for improving group management techniques.

(1) An officer should try to get to know himself. He should do this, not as was mentioned earlier by reading one of the popular paper-backs on *How to Psycho-analyse Yourself*, but by answering the four questions posed at the end of the first chapter: What am I doing, why am I doing it, where am I going, and how am I going to get there? Once an officer has answered these questions he will be able to increase his feeling of importance for the job and will become more enthusiastic. This enthusiasm will be picked up by his juniors and the whole group will work all the more efficiently. One of the most potent tools in leadership is personal example; that is why officers should be continuously striving to improve themselves and to increase their enthusiasm for the work in hand.

An officer may hold what views he likes about his current employers but, if these are unfavourable, he should keep them to himself and not voice them when in the hearing of the crew. How can the crew be expected to give of their best if the officers are forever running down the Company who own the ship?

(2) An officer, particularly a senior officer, should try to put himself in his junior's place and feel with him. Most officers should be able to remember how they felt on the way up; how, as first trippers, they stood in awe of the Master, the Chief Engineer or the Chief Officer. An officer, holding a senior position, should remember that that is how the juniors now feel about him. Senior

officers should make allowances for their juniors and should try to help these younger men preserve their individuality and keep their self-respect.

It is important to encourage original thought in all men so that, when a junior comes out with a suggested way of doing a particular job, the senior officer should implement this idea if he can or show the junior the weaknesses in his suggested plan if another method is to be adopted. If a senior officer wants his juniors to be interested in his ideas, he must show that he is interested in their views.

(3) No Master or senior officer should submerge himself in detail while the rest of the enterprise fails through lack of control. This type of failure can be guarded against by the Master and senior officers delegating work to those below instead of trying to deal with every little thing that crops up. The senior officer must tell his junior exactly what his duties and responsibilities are and what authority he has to carry out these tasks. The junior must be told exactly what is expected of him and what he must do; he should not be left to do what he thinks he should. When delegating work to others, the senior must make quite clear what feed-back of information he requires.

Many Masters are criticized for not delegating more work to their officers, yet is this criticism fair? So long as Masters feel that they will be held responsible for all accidents they will be reluctant to delegate work to others, particularly in the navigational field. It is up to shipping companies to encourage their Masters to delegate certain work to others provided, of course, the officers concerned are competent and experienced. It would be foolhardy of a Master to expect an inexperienced Third Officer to take the ship through a narrow and dangerous waterway. On the other hand, it is equally foolhardy of a Master to stay on the bridge in restricted visibility for two or three days on end when his experienced Chief Officer could easily carry out this task for him. It is more important for the Master to be fresh and alert for the really congested waterways where emergencies may arise than for him to stay on the bridge for days on end in relatively open areas.

Most officers would agree that the happiest ships are those on which they feel that they have a real job of work to do. What possible interest can a young officer have in the navigation of the ship when he is instructed to call the Master for every alteration in course, no matter how small it may be? On the other hand, a young officer who has been ordered to carry out the necessary alterations of course at particular positions will take a far greater interest in the navigation of the ship and, once he has made an alteration, he will enjoy the pride that comes from a job well done. Most officers call for more work and responsibility to be delegated to them yet, in many cases, those officers who are most vociferous on this point are the ones who delegate least when they eventually get command.

Delegation of work and responsibilities to others is a habit that can be cultivated from an early age and, unless a man has cultivated this habit while still an officer, he is unlikely to start delegating responsibility to others once he reaches command. Some junior officers would argue that because of the nature of their work, they have no scope for developing this habit. Such is not the case and an example will illustrate what can be done by a junior officer.

Take, for example, a tanker in port with a Third Officer and cadet on cargo watch. At a particular instant, a valve on the fore-deck may have to be opened. The Third Officer has three courses of action open to him: He could go forward and open the valve himself, or he could take the cadet forward with him and order the cadet to open the valve in his presence, or he could stay where he is and order the cadet to go forward alone to open the valve. Whatever happens the valve must be opened for, otherwise, the pipeline may burst with disastrous results and the Third Officer will be held responsible. If the Third Officer goes forward to the valve he will gain peace of mind but neither he nor the cadet will gain in experience. If, however, the Third Officer chooses the third course of action and instructs the cadet to open the valve alone, then the cadet will derive satisfaction from being entrusted with an important job and the Third

Officer will have taken one step towards gaining confidence in others.

At a very junior level, an officer can use the cadets to improve his delegation techniques but, as he is promoted to high rank, he can extend his delegation of work to the other officers and to the crew. In time he will gain confidence in himself and his juniors and should prove to be a good Master when he reaches command.

(4) An officer, or any man for that matter, should never be afraid to admit that he does not know something or that he is unable to answer a particular question. He should, however, try to avoid repeating this admission by keeping up to date with technical progress in the shipping industry. Once they obtain their certificates, some Masters and officers lose all interest in increasing their technical knowledge, with the result that the first they hear of a new navigational device is when workmen come aboard to fit that device in their ships.

Apart from not being prepared for new navigational and engineering devices, some officers, who have not kept up to date with modern trends, are prone to scoff at new subjects being studied by their cadets. This retards the progress of an individual cadet and, indeed, it retards the progress of the whole Merchant Navy.

(5) A Master or officer should raise individual and group morale by recognizing and praising the efforts of those below. If ratings who show above-average ability or devotion to duty get no special treatment or recognition, they will wonder if the extra effort was worthwhile and will gradually fall back to the common level of the rest of the crew.

(6) A weakness of some officers is that they cannot walk around the ship without urging the crew to hurry up. As they pass each group of men they come out with phrases like "Can't you do it quicker than that?" or "Haven't you finished that job yet?" More often than not, these never-ending urges to hurry up come from bad habit on the officer's part, and any man suffering from this weakness should try to overcome it. Continual nagging simply fills the crew with nervousness or resentment.

(7) An officer should never confuse a disciplinary problem with a personal situation. This is best illustrated by an example. On a particular ship there was a Third Officer who was not very efficient and who did not display much interest in his work. He often left the bridge in an untidy state or he did not check the lifeboat equipment thoroughly even though he was ordered to do so. The ship arrived in port and the mail came on board. As usually happens, there were one or two letters for the rest of the crew and about twenty letters for the Third Officer (Third Officers are always in love!) The Master, in handing out the mail said to the Third Officer "Here is your mail but you don't deserve it", and in saying this he confused the disciplinary with the personal situation. The Third Officer should, of course, have been reprimanded for his dereliction of duty, but the Master's remarks on his mail were unnecessary and hurtful; the letters were something quite personal between this young officer and his girl friend.

(8) Officers should beware of dangerous subjects when talking to their subordinates. Officers should, of course, draw free comment from others and, in open waters, should be prepared to talk to the man on the wheel. But the subject of discussion should be such that neither the officer nor the man will get emotionally worked up. For example, a discussion on the relative merits of the two major political parties in Britain may develop into a violent argument between the officer and the rating and will be brought to an abrupt end when the officer reprimands the rating for being off course!

(9) Men like to see their head at ease, not trying to win favour by acting like a fool. On one ship, the Master used to hurl himself out of the wheelhouse every time an aeroplane flew overhead. He would lie prostrate on the wing of the bridge and make a noise like a machine gun. At the time everyone laughed dutifully, but lying flat on the bridge wing was not quite the right place for the Master of the ship, and the discipline on board suffered.

It need hardly be mentioned that officers should never play practical jokes on their subordinates. On one day an officer on the bridge may think it funny to pour a bucket of soojee on a rating below, but next day, that same rating, working aloft, may pour a tin of paint onto the officer. A violent stream of mutual abuse will probably follow, with the officer accusing the rating of being impertinent and insolent.

(10) Once an order has been issued, the officer should give the men time to complete the work involved before issuing another order. Provided this is done, the crew will accept that the work has been well planned. If, on the other hand, a man is told to do one thing and then, before he has had time to finish it, is ordered to do some other work, he simply becomes irritated and becomes convinced that the officer does not know his own mind.

An example will illustrate this. A ship was due to arrive at Port Said at noon. At 0900 the Chief Officer should have told the crew to get the mooring ropes ready but he forgot to do so and instructed them to paint the bridge front bulkhead instead. No sooner had the crew got their stages rigged and had started to paint when the Chief Officer remembered the ropes. He rushed out on deck, stopped their work, and told them to prepare the ropes. In that particular case, the Chief Officer would have been better advised to have waited until a natural break in the work, for example smokho, and then instructed the crew to prepare the ropes before returning to their painting.

A worker should never be told that the work he is doing—and which is the result of an order given to him—is unimportant and that he should be doing something else.

Example. At 0700 the Chief Officer could not think what work to give the cadets to do, so instructed them to clean the wheelhouse windows. They started on this job, and then at 0730 the Chief Officer suddenly remembered that the sounding machine had to be opened up for overhaul by the Second Officer. He put his head out over the bridge wing and said to the apprentices, "You are wasting your time on cleaning windows. Go aft to open up the sounding machine." The apprentices naturally wondered why they had been told to clean the windows if this job was a waste of time.

(11) An officer should always use the results of an order he has given and not wait until the man has finished the job before telling him that he has wasted his time.

Example. A ship was in port. The Master called up the Second Officer and told him to get figures on the total steaming times and bunkers consumed for the previous year. The Second Officer went off, got out all the log-books and bunker statements, prepared a rough copy of the figures, and then wrote out a fair copy. He took an hour or two and was proud of what he did. He returned to the Master's room only to be greeted by the Master saying "You took too long; I've made up some figures, they will do." The Second Officer went away feeling very deflated and rather angry that his whole morning had been wasted. In the example quoted here the Master should either have made up the figures in the first place (if approximate figures were suitable) or he should have accepted the Second Officer's figures with a word of thanks.

CHAPTER 5

Man Management

MAN management concerns the face-to-face situation which arises between employer and employee, between manager and worker, or between officer and rating. There are both good and bad ways of issuing orders and reprimands and, once again, it must be emphasized that an officer should try to develop those techniques which will best suit his personality. Some officers may succeed with an abrupt, clipped approach while others may find that a softer manner is more effective. It is worth mentioning, however, that we are living in a democratic and not in an autocratic society.

Some officers at sea today may deplore the apparent indiscipline of some of their ratings and could probably support their views with a great deal of evidence. Such officers should recognize that home, school and industrial discipline has changed from what it was at the turn of the century and that modern recruits to the Merchant Navy come from a democratic society which possibly errs on the side of being too permissive. Many recruits find it difficult to knuckle down to the autocratic system aboard ship and may resent the old-fashioned methods of order giving and punishment. Just as the workers do not control a factory ashore, the crew do not control a ship. The officers are in charge and it is their duty to get the best out of their ratings by managing them properly.

In order that an officer may develop sound ways of issuing orders and reprimands, it is essential that he understands the reasons why men obey or disobey orders.

Obedience

There are many reasons why men obey orders and one of these reasons is fear of punishment. In a dictatorship, or in a country occupied by a foreign army, fear of punishment may be the only way of getting some sort of obedience to orders. Fear, however, will never get the wholehearted co-operation of the workers. If workers are really afraid of the order giver they will relieve their fear and resentment by engaging in surreptitious activities aimed at destroying their controlling authority. There was ample evidence of this in the occupied countries during the war.

As was mentioned in the previous chapter, workers resent too much harshness. If the officers of a ship are too harsh, or if the crew go in fear of punishment, the crew members may relieve their feelings of hatred or resentment by destroying equipment or by wasting stores. They will certainly not enter into the full spirit of securing the successful trading of the ship. Threat of punishment, therefore, is not the ideal way of securing obedience to orders on board a ship.

Apart from fear of punishment, there are four main reasons why people obey orders.

(1) They may obey for emotional reasons; they may love, esteem, or have strong feelings of loyalty towards the order giver. An extreme form of this type of obedience is that displayed by a husband when his wife puts her cold foot in the middle of his back and says "Tea". He jumps out of bed and makes the morning tea simply because he loves his wife!

Ratings, however, are not madly in love with their officers but they may really respect a particular officer and, as a result, will probably obey his orders cheerfully and without question. Most seamen will have seen this type of obedience in action when serving in a ship with a very popular Master or officer. The popular officer can get the crew to do almost anything. From the officer's point of view, however, the disadvantage of being too popular is that his success with the crew may be resented by the rest of the officers and, in particular, by his senior officers.

Research carried out in the U.S. Navy showed that the closer an officer became to the crew, the greater the gulf became between him and the rest of the officers. Another disadvantage of being too popular is that, in port, such an officer runs the risk of being awakened in the early hours of the morning by happy ratings on their return from shore leave who insist on that officer joining them for a drink!

(2) Some men obey orders because of their own weakness; they obey an order to secure future protection from the order giver. An extreme example of this type of obedience was the obedience given to Al Capone by his gangsters. They carried out Capone's orders without question, but when they themselves were attacked, they turned to Capone for protection. On a much less extreme plane, we see this type of obedience in ships and an example may be used to illustrate this point.

We may have a young junior engineer who has just joined his first ship. He may not understand the full set-up and may have been led to believe that the Master, Chief Officer and Chief Steward are all hard men who, at the slightest provocation, will make life very unpleasant for this young engineer. At the same time, this young engineer recognizes that the Second Engineer is his working boss and his potential protector. If now the Second Engineer enters this young engineer's cabin and asks him to go to the Chief Steward and get a case of beer, the young engineer will obey this order or request simply to buy future protection from the Second Engineer even though the fetching of beer is not one of his duties as a junior engineer.

(3) Some men obey orders because it suits their own ends. This is calculated obedience and is, sometimes, dangerous. Take, for example, a Second Officer who wants permission from the Master for his fiancée to visit him in the next port. (Second Officers always have fiancées, Third Officers have girl friends!) During the week or month or two before asking for this permission, the Second Officer may obey every order from the Master cheerfully, quickly and without question just so that his request will be viewed in a favourable light. Once this officer has had his request

granted, and no longer needs to gain the approval of the Master, he may cease to be quite so ready to obey orders and, indeed, may endanger the ship by failing to carry out an order that the Master assumed would be obeyed.

(4) Best of all is the obedience that is given by intelligent men who realize that orders are necessary. They almost ignore the personality of the order giver and simply get on with the job. A good example of this is the order given to the crew to stand by fore and aft when the ship approaches her berth in port. The crew know that they are needed to help moor the ship and it does not really matter who tells them to stand by—an officer, bosun or cadet—they simply pick up their gloves and coats and go to their stations. Officers should try to obtain this type of obedience for all their orders, and they will go a long way towards achieving this if they keep the crew fully informed on all that is going on and on the plan of work that has been decided upon.

Disobedience

While it is important to understand the main reasons for obedience, it is equally as important to understand why some men disobey orders. As with obedience, there are many reasons for disobedience and some of the more important reasons are given below.

(1) A man may disobey an order because he is asocial; he feels that he is not a member of a particular group and, therefore, has no wish to contribute towards that group's success. An example may help to illustrate this type of disobedience.

A group of firemen (under the Second Engineer) were engaged in lifting a spare part on board by means of a single davit and a tackle. The part was heavy and they were having some difficulty. Standing near by was a sailor drinking his morning coffee. The Second Engineer asked this sailor to help heave on the tackle but he refused to do so and moved away muttering that he was not a fireman.

(2) Another man may disobey for antisocial reasons. He may

be employed as a member of a particular group but, because the rest of the group has angered or hurt him in some way, he does all he can to prevent the group achieving its goal.

(3) Still another reason for disobedience is that a man may have an exaggerated sense of his own importance and feel that the work he has been ordered to do is beneath his dignity. This type of disobedience is not uncommon in modern society where men are given fancy titles and where they are sometimes given the wrong idea during recruitment as a result of which they feel that they should not have to do menial tasks.

(4) Others disobey because of a sense of inferiority; through disobedience they try to show the order giver that they are as good as he is. Sometimes this sense of inferiority comes from a physical handicap which may be nothing more than lack of height. When a short man appears to be "cocky" he is simply adopting aggressive or cheeky attitudes in order to show the world that he is as good as the taller men around him.

(5) Finally, there is the disobedience which arises when a man simply dislikes the job he has been ordered to do.

There are of course, various grades of disobedience. At one extreme there is outright disobedience when a man absolutely refuses to obey an order. At the other extreme is the situation where a man has carried out an order in such a poor or half-hearted way that his actions are tantamount to disobedience of the spirit of the order. Officers should be able to gauge the degree of disobedience and should try to determine the possible reasons for this behaviour before reprimanding or punishing the man. The failure to carry out an order cannot always be blamed on the rating for he may not have understood just what the officer wanted him to do; it is absolutely essential that an officer gives his orders in the correct manner.

Orders

(1) Only well-considered orders should be given. No good at all comes from an officer hesitating and correcting his order out

loud, for it simply irritates the man waiting to take the order. "I'm thinking aloud", says the officer. "Doesn't know his own mind", thinks the rating.

Example. A Master called a cadet up to his cabin to give him an order, and said, "Now go to the Chief Officer and tell him to put the special cargo. . . . No, go to the Chief Steward first and tell him I . . . No, I know, go to the Chief Engineer first and tell him. . . . No, scrub all that. Go to the Chief Officer first and tell him to put the special cargo in number 3 hatch." After all this, the cadet just did not know what he was supposed to do.

(2) The order should not be open to criticism by conflicting with something the order giver, himself, said the previous day.

Example. A ship was in port and, at lunch time, the Third Officer was on deck with a cadet dressed in his working gear. An emergency cropped up and the Third Officer told the cadet to get the Chief Officer who, at that time, was in the saloon. The cadet rushed into the saloon but before he could talk to the Chief Officer, the Master bellowed at him and told him not to come into the saloon in such dirty clothes. The cadet had to stand at the doorway and ask a steward to pass a message to the Chief Officer. Next morning, the cadet was, once again, on deck in his working clothes, the Master was on the deck above and the Chief Officer was in the saloon having breakfast. The Master wanted the Chief Officer so ordered the cadet to get the Chief Officer. The cadet did not move away immediately and, when asked what was causing his hesitation, the cadet replied that he was in working clothes and, complying with what the Master had said the previous day, he could not go into the saloon. "Oh, forget that," said the Master, "just go into the saloon and tell the Chief Officer I want him." This bending of rules to suit the order giver upsets the order taker and causes resentment.

(3) Orders should be given clearly and precisely in as few words as possible.

(4) The order should sound convincing and, when time permits, the order taker should be put in the picture so that he understands the reasons for the order.

Example. A ship coming in to port was approaching the pilot vessel. The officer on watch called up the stand-by man and gruffly said, "Get the pilot ladder over the port side." A better way of issuing this particular order would have been for the officer to have called up the rating, pointed to the pilot vessel, and mentioned that they would be close to it in about ten minutes and that the pilot ladder should be rigged on the port side. The rating would then know why he had to rig the pilot ladder and how his particular task fitted in with all that was going on around him.

(5) A man should only be given the minimum number of orders in order to prevent mental overloading. Quite often a man is accused of disobedience or of forgetting to do something when the fault really lies with the order giver in issuing too many orders at one time.

Example. A Master called up a cadet and, having marshalled his thoughts beforehand, said, "Tell the Chief Officer that I want to see him. Then tell the Chief Steward that three officials are staying for lunch. Then tell the Second Steward that the laundry must go ashore this morning. Then go to the Chief Engineer and get the bunker book and then tell the Second Engineer that the bunker barge is coming alongside at noon. And, by the way, tell the electrician that the light on my desk has failed and I would like him to fix it as soon as possible." The poor cadet went away mentally reeling. He remembered the first few jobs but forgot to tell the electrician about the desk light which needed repair. Later, the cadet was reprimanded by the Master for being a ,orgetful boy with no interest in the ship or in his own job. There was very little the cadet could say in reply.

(6) Verbal orders should only be given to the man who has to do the job. Much better than the Master telling a cadet to tell the Chief Officer to put the special cargo in number 3 hatch would be for the Master either to send a written note to the Chief Officer or to order the cadet to tell the Chief Officer that he was wanted by the Master.

Some shipping companies have adopted an excellent system of

an order book over and above the standard "night order book". Every important order from the Master or Watchkeeping Officer to someone else in the ship is entered in this book and is initialled by the person who has to execute the order.

(7) There should be no ambiguity in orders. It is the duty of the order giver to decide what is to be done and the order in which the various jobs should be done.

Example. A ship was approaching an anchorage. The officer on the bridge called the stand-by man and said, "Get in the log and call the Chief Officer." The rating did not know whether there was sufficient time for him to get in the log before calling the Chief Officer or whether he should call the Chief Officer before dealing with the log. He asked the officer what he should do first. "I don't care," replied the officer, "just get in the log and call the Mate." This was quite wrong of the officer, for the rating was left in a quandary. He could not be sure that there was time to call the Chief Officer before getting in the log in case the engines were put astern and the log fouled in the propeller. On the other hand, if he dealt with the log first, the ship may have arrived at her anchorage position before the Chief Officer reached the focs'le head. In the example used here, and in any other similar situation, the order in which jobs are to be carried out must be made quite clear by the order giver.

(8) All orders should be given in a calm, clear manner. While difficult to do at certain times, the habit of using a calm voice for all orders is one worth cultivating. All men, and particularly sailors, respect a cool hand.

If an order is not carried out then the most important thing for the officer to do is to *keep calm*. He should then try to find out why the order was not carried out and only after getting all the facts should he give extra orders or reprimand the man. Angry outbursts do no good at all, neither to the order giver nor to the order taker. A subordinate should *always* be given a chance to explain why he did not or could not carry out the order given to him for, if an officer starts shouting and reproving the man before he has all the facts, he may end up looking rather silly.

If a subordinate or rating has no valid explanation for failing to carry out the order he should be reprimanded. There are various ways by which a man may be reprimanded and speaking the naked truth in a cold and dispassionate voice is not always the best way. Masters and officers should remember at all times that their duty is to get the best out of the men under their control and not simply to act as dispensers of punishment.

People resent censure for it deflates their sense of self-importance, yet, when the circumstances of the case warrant it, men must be reprimanded for disobedience. Some Masters and officers say nothing when a job has been well done yet they criticize at great length when work has not been done to their satisfaction. Many a young officer can probably recall making a mistake and then having the Master reproach him throughout the morning watch, during the meal reliefs and again throughout the evening watch. A man receiving such a lengthy reproof soon builds up a feeling of resentment and hatred for his superior. It is advisable to deliver reprimands in as few words as possible.

An officer should never shrink from criticizing one man while censuring another weaker man for the same offence. It is a fairly common human failing for a man to project his own weaknesses onto those he despises, and an officer therefore should try to avoid over-criticizing those men he likes least. The main point to grasp, however, is that an officer should never shirk reprimanding one man while severely reprimanding another for the same offence.

Take as an example something that has happened to most of us at one time or another. A ship in port was ready to sail. The pilot was on board and the tugs were made fast, yet the sailing was delayed by the absence of two men who were in a dockside pub slaking their thirst! After a while they came into sight walking slowly back to the ship. Nothing could have been more infuriating than the slowness of their gait. One of them was a big, tough fireman, the other a small little deck boy. The Master shouted at them to hurry up. The deck boy was seen to start hurrying but was soon slowed down again by the bigger man, who refused to hurry. As they came up the gangway the Master called them up to the bridge. The big tough fireman refused to come, on the grounds that he was going on watch. The deck boy, trembling a little, went up to the Master. The Master gave vent to his feelings by severely reprimanding the deck boy. The boy became filled with resentment for he felt that the Master was shouting at him because of his small size and yet this same Master was afraid to reprimand the bigger, tougher fireman.

When criticizing or reprimanding a man, an officer should not come out with a lot of generalizations but should be as precise as possible. The offender should be left in no doubt as to what he has done wrong and how the situation may be rectified. The officer should always say how the job should have been done.

Personal remarks should be excluded from reprimands. For example, a Master should never say "This is no good for *me*" or "Why do *I* have to put up with people like you?"

Before reprimanding a man, an officer should make sure that he has all the facts of the case and that the reprimand is deserved. An unjust reprimand causes long-lasting harm. When dealing with an over-sensitive man or with a young boy, an officer should try to temper his criticism and should end the reprimand with some placable remarks.

When the non-execution of an order has caused great personal inconvenience to an officer, anger is understandable but not excusable. Ranting, raving, and shouting are supposed to inspire fear in the subordinate: it may have done so years ago, but not today. This type of behaviour in an officer will earn him nothing but contempt from his ratings and juniors. Sometimes the officer's loss of temper shows that he fears those he is reprimanding. If an officer does lose his temper, he should break off the interview and deal with the matter some time later when he is in a calmer frame of mind.

There are many methods of criticism and an officer should study the man first before deciding what course of action to adopt. No officer should use the same approach at all times, for his choice of phrases will soon become well known and will be mimicked in the sailors' mess!

(1) There is the tactful approach where the superior mixes criticism of the current misdemeanour with praise for past work well done.

Example. We could consider the position of a Master when he finds that the Second Officer has neglected to maintain the echo sounder. The Master could reprimand the Second Officer harshly and clearly by saying, "Why the hell haven't you looked after the echo sounder? You know it is your job to do so. I am damn well going to report you to the Company." On the other hand the Master could reprimand the officer by saying, "Well, Second Mate, you have always looked after the gyro well, you've always kept the charts up to date, but you have completely neglected the echo sounder . . . and now we are aground."

(2) There is the disguised approach when, in the hearing of the man who should have done the job, the superior remarks that it has not been done.

Example. A Master, on Sunday rounds of the ship with his senior officers, noticed that a scupper was blocked in the firemen's bathroom. He instructed the Chief Officer to have it cleared. During rounds a week later, the Master noticed that the scupper was still blocked. He could have turned on the Chief Officer and reprimanded him for dereliction of duty. Instead, he mentioned, out loud, "That's funny, I thought I noticed this last week. Never mind. Mister Jones, would you get this scupper cleared, please?" Now, in adopting this method, the Master had given the Chief Officer a way out. If the Chief Officer really had carried out the first order to have the scupper cleared but it had become blocked again, he could tell the Master that he had done so. On the other hand, if the Chief Officer had overlooked this particular job, he would make sure that it was dealt with immediately for he would be aware of the fact that the Master *knew* that the blocked scupper had been mentioned during rounds the previous week.

(3) Still another method of reprimand is for the superior to ask the offender if anything is wrong.

Example. A Second Officer had always carried out his duties in an exemplary manner. After leaving a certain port, the Master noticed that this officer was neglecting some of his work, had taken to having an extra gin before lunch, and was not paying as much attention as he should to his dress. In this situation, the Master could have severely reprimanded the Second Officer and could have told him to pull himself together. Instead, the Master asked the Second Officer if anything was wrong; and found out that this officer had just had a letter from his fiancée to say that he had better get home as soon as possible to marry her!

(4) With all intelligent subordinates it should be possible to discuss, quite openly, the facts of the disobedience or of the neglect of duty. The Master or officer should say clearly what the subordinate should have done, what effects his disobedience have had on the ship and whether or not an adverse report would be made on this man's conduct.

As was mentioned in the chapter dealing with supervision, it is far better to reprimand a man for a number of faults at one time than to nag at him continuously.

In general, it is best never to threaten a man with some form of punishment if he does something a second time. If a man has been disobedient then, depending on the circumstances of the case, he should be reprimanded or punished; after which the matter should be closed. If, however, an officer decides not to punish the man for the first offence but threatens to punish him for a repetition of the same offence then the officer has put himself in a very vulnerable position. In so many cases, the repetition of the offence is associated with extenuating circumstances which again makes the officer decide not to punish the man. The man concerned, having got away with a repetition of the offence, will start thinking that the officer is weak or is afraid to punish him. He will simply continue with his offences against discipline.

Any man who wants to command well *must* learn to punish well, and must never shirk this unpleasant duty. If an officer or Master does not punish offenders he simply undermines his own authority.

CHAPTER 6

Punishment

UNLESS he suffers from some psychological abnormality, no man really enjoys punishing another, yet, as was mentioned at the end of the last chapter, any officer who wants to command well must learn to punish all offenders against discipline.

There are many differences between the Royal and Merchant Navies but the most notable one concerns discipline. Some people would argue that, while a rigid system of discipline and punishments is needed in the Royal Navy in order to train men for complete obedience to orders in time of war, no rigid system is required in merchant ships and that all punishment should be abolished. People who argue in this way overlook the fact that in both naval and merchant ships large groups of men have to live and work together in very confined spaces and, unless a strict code of discipline exists, disharmony and inefficiency are bound to result.

In the Royal Navy, descriptions of offences and the punishment for each are laid down in the Queen's Regulations and Admiralty Instructions. Punishments are administered impersonally, for each man in the Royal Navy knows what punishment is laid down for each offence and that Commanding Officers have little discretion in the matter.

In the Merchant Navy, descriptions of offences and the punishment for each are contained in the Articles of Agreement for each ship and in the Merchant Shipping Act 1894. However, all Merchant Navy Masters and officers do not interpret these offences in the same way, with the result that in one ship a man may be fined a day's pay for a particular offence while in another ship he may be let off with nothing more than a slight reprimand for exactly the same offence; the punishment a man gets depends almost entirely on the discretion of his senior officers. This lack of uniformity of punishment for offences makes it hard for both Masters and ratings; neither knows exactly where they stand when an offence has been committed. If discipline in the Merchant Navy is to be improved there must be a completely uniform interpretation of offences and punishments throughout all merchant ships.

Once a man has been in command for a number of years, he will have worked out his own methods of dealing with offenders, but a younger Master, doing his first voyage in command, may not have had the time or experience to work out his own code. In this case, he may find it helpful to list all possible offences against discipline and the punishment he proposes to give for each. He could keep this list for personal reference or, better still, he may display it on the crew's notice board. He must then take great care to administer the punishments he has listed to all offenders no matter what their station. In this way punishments will be fair and will be seen to be fair.

One of the most difficult problems facing a Master, particularly a young Master, is the disciplining of his officers. While the Master needs the whole-hearted co-operation of his officers to secure the efficient running of the ship, he should make it quite clear that the rules of conduct and discipline will be applied more strictly to the officers than to the ratings. How, in all fairness, can a Master punish a rating for, say, being drunk, when the rating can point to an officer who escaped punishment for the same offence?

Most officers respect a Master who has the ability and courage to punish offenders against discipline for they find their own jobs are made easier; they feel that they have the backing of the Master in relation to disciplinary problems. (How many Chief Officers have gnashed their teeth when, on taking a man before the Master for punishment, the man has been let off with nothing more than a mild reprimand?) If officers want the backing of the Master in disciplinary problems then they, too, must be prepared to comply with whatever code of conduct has been laid down.

A Master, or officer, when punishing a man should try to avoid using the first person singular. Rather than say, "You were drunk therefore *I* am going to fine you one day's pay" he should say, "As a result of your being drunk you delayed the ship or someone else had to do your work. You will, therefore, be fined a day's pay."

Punishment should be a real deterrent against repetition of the offence and should not be aimed at inspiring fear in the rating. In ships in which high overtime payments can be earned, standard fines of one or two days' pay for the offences listed in the Articles are not always effective in preventing repetition of the offences. More effective forms of punishment may be to withold overtime work from the offender or to order that the offender is to be given no advances on his wages in the next port or ports. One effective method of instilling discipline in a crew is for the Master to make a log entry, but not apply the fine, on the first occasion a man offends against discipline. If the man subsequently repeats the offence, it becomes a second offence and a higher fine is applicable.

It is absolutely essential that a Master gets all the facts of a case before punishing a man. Some men become tongue-tied when in the presence of the Master and are unable to explain their side of the case while others, through over-use of those words not normally used in polite company, cannot express themselves plainly and the Master is left without a clear understanding of their side of the case. It is important for the Master to draw these men out as much as possible and there may be merit in the suggestion made in the Pearson Report,[20] that all offenders should be accompanied by a "friend" when summoned before the Master for punishment.

If various other recommendations of the Pearson Report are implemented there may be changes in the Merchant Shipping Acts and different forms of punishment may be introduced. As things are today, a Master has a number of ways of punishing an offender.

(1) **Logging on board ship**

In the Articles of Agreement, the following offences are listed:

(a) Striking or assaulting any person on board or belonging to the ship.

(b) Bringing or having intoxicating liquors on board.

(c) Drunkenness.

(d) Taking on board or having in possession any offensive weapon without the Master's consent.

(e) Insolent or contemptuous language to the Master or any officer.

(f) Disobedience of any lawful command.

(g) Absence without leave.

The penalties for each of the above are one day's pay for the first offence and two days' pay for second and subsequent offences. In addition to these fines, a man may be forced to forfeit a day's pay for each day on which he failed to report for duty. These forfeitures are based on the principle of "No work: No pay" and are not, therefore, fines or punishments in the true sense of the word.

In order to apply one of these fines to an offender, the details of the offence and the fine to be applied must be entered in the official log book and read out to the offender in the presence of a witness. The man's reply, if any, must be entered in the log book and the whole entry signed by the Master or officer and by the witness. Under Section 228 of the Merchant Shipping Act 1894, any log entry for an offence against discipline which has occurred at sea must be made before the vessel arrives at her next port; if the offence occurs in port, the entry must be made before the ship puts to sea. A certain amount of leeway is allowed for, if the ship is on the point of sailing when the offence occurs, the log entry may be made as soon as possible after the ship puts to sea.

As the law stands today, the offender has no right to appoint a spokesman to act on his behalf but, as was mentioned previously, one of the recommendations of the Pearson Report[20] was that the offender should have the right to invite a "friend" to accompany him before the Master when the logging procedure is carried out. The "friend" should be someone who can help and advise the offender.

Subsequent good behaviour on the part of the offender may make the Master wish to cancel the fine and log entry. The Master may do this by making another entry in the log book to the effect that owing to the subsequent good behaviour of (name of seaman and rating), the entry and fine made on page (number to be given) is now cancelled. This entry must be signed by the Master and one other person.

The Master's power to cancel fines should only be used with the greatest discretion and only when the circumstances of the case really warrant it. Much of the indiscipline in the Merchant Service today is due to the habit of some Masters who cancel all loggings at the end of a voyage almost as a matter of course. Any Master who cancels a fine automatically shows his weakness and his inability to punish. In turn, ratings who escape punishment in this way cease to attach any importance to loggings on future ships, with the result that indiscipline is almost encouraged. A Master who cancels loggings automatically at the end of a voyage not only shows his weakness and his inability to punish, but he lets down all his fellow Masters throughout the rest of the Merchant Service.

(2) Punishment by courts ashore

Section 225 of the Merchant Shipping Act 1894[13]
General offences against discipline

If a seaman lawfully engaged or an apprentice to the sea service commits any of the following offences, in this Act referred to as offences against discipline, he shall be liable to be punished summarily as follows: that is to say,

(a) If he quits the ship without leave after her arrival at her port of delivery, and before she is placed in security, he shall be liable to forfeit out of his wages a sum not exceeding one month's pay.

(b) If he is guilty of wilful disobedience to any lawful command he shall be liable to imprisonment for a period not exceeding four weeks, and also, at the discretion of the court, to forfeit out of his wages a sum not exceeding two days' pay.

(c) If he is guilty of continued wilful disobedience to lawful commands or continued wilful neglect of duty, he shall be liable to imprisonment for a period not exceeding twelve weeks, and also, at the discretion of the court, to forfeit for every twenty-four hours' continuance of disobedience or neglect, either a sum not exceeding six days' pay or any expenses properly incurred in hiring a substitute.

(d) If he assaults the Master or any Mate or certificated engineer of the ship, he shall be liable to imprisonment for a period not exceeding twelve weeks.

(e) If he combines with any of the crew to disobey lawful commands, or to neglect duty, or to impede the navigation of the ship or the progress of the voyage, he shall be liable to imprisonment for a period not exceeding twelve weeks.

(f) If he wilfully damages his ship, or embezzles or wilfully damages any of her stores or cargo, he shall be liable to forfeit out of his wages a sum equal to the loss thereby sustained, and also, at the discretion of the court, to imprisonment for a period not exceeding twelve weeks.

(g) If he is convicted of any act of smuggling, whereby loss or damage is occasioned to the Master or owner of the ship, he shall be liable to pay to that Master or owner a sum sufficient to reimburse the loss or damage; and the whole or a proportionate part of his wages may be retained in satisfaction or on account of that liability, without prejudice to any further remedy.

Any Master who wishes to take a man before a court for one of the offences listed should make sure of two things:

(1) The official log book must contain full details of the offence, supported by signed statements of witnesses if necessary.

(2) The man must not already have been fined on board for

the offence for which he is to be taken before the court ashore. This is because of our British legal principle of not punishing a man twice for the same offence.

The two most common reasons for Masters bringing men before courts ashore are for continued disobedience of lawful commands or for continued absence from duty. In these cases, a Master may make a number of log entries about a particular man, and fine him for the first and some of the subsequent offences. If, after continued disobedience, the Master decides to take the man before a court, he should not fine the man for the last one or two repetitions of this offence but should make log entries stating that the man has been disobedient or absent without leave and that the case will be taken before a court on return to the United Kingdom or in some other suitable country.

Many Masters hesitate to take offenders before a court as they know it will mean a loss of some of their leave and that their companies may not like the adverse publicity which stems from court cases. Shipping companies should help their Masters in this respect by making clear their views on these court actions and by making good any losses a Master suffers in respect of leave and expenses.

The remedies contained in Section 225 are falling into disuse nowadays for a speedier method of dealing with an offender exists in the Merchant Navy Establishment Scheme described later in this book.

(3) Punishment of officers

Certificated officers are not fined on board in the same way as are ratings and uncertificated officers for misconduct or offences against discipline. Instead, they may be summoned before a Court of Inquiry into the Conduct of a Certificated Officer. This court has the power to recommend the suspension or cancellation of certificates of competency.

If an officer fails to carry out the lawful commands of the Master, or if he executes his duty in a dangerous manner, or if he appears to be intoxicated when required for duty, or if he commits any other offence against discipline, the Master should make a full entry in the official log book, giving details of the offence and supported by statements from witnesses if necessary. The offence must then be reported to the Board of Trade who will then convene the Court of Inquiry. This is held at a port in the United Kingdom, although if the ship's articles are opened and closed in a British port abroad, a preliminary inquiry may be held at that port by a Superintendent of a Mercantile Marine office or by some other proper authority.

(4) Reports of conduct and ability in discharge books

In accordance with the Merchant Shipping Acts, every seaman discharged from a British ship must be given a certificate of discharge. This is usually contained in the seaman's discharge book. The Master actually records his reports of conduct and ability in the front pages of the official log book and these reports are subsequently copied into the discharge books by the official before whom the crew are discharged.

The standard report is V.G. (Very Good) for both conduct and ability, although G. (Good) is sometimes used. Under the system of reports as they are today, V.G. means nothing more than satisfactory and G. is usually taken to mean something slightly less than satisfactory.

If a Master is dissatisfied with a man's conduct or ability, then he inserts D.R. (Decline to Report) under the appropriate headings. This is taken as a bad discharge or as a black mark and is a form of punishment, for a man with D.R. in his discharge book may find it difficult to obtain employment in certain ships in the future. Under the present system a man can escape this form of punishment by "losing" his discharge book and applying to the Registrar General of Shipping and Seamen for a new one. The D.R. report is not entered in his new book.

The Pearson Report[20] has recommended that bad reports should only be issued by a shore tribunal before whom the man will have the right of defending himself and against whom the man will have the right of appeal. Once this tribunal has issued or confirmed a bad report it will be entered in the man's records and will appear in all future discharge books issued to him.

In addition to the three types of reports already described, there is a fourth type of report which is sometimes entered in a man's discharge book. A man may, if he wishes, ask the official before whom he is discharged to enter the words "Endorsement not required" in his discharge book. When this entry appears under the "conduct" column, it is usually taken as a bad discharge and that the man avoided having the entry D.R. simply by asking for this particular endorsement.

Both officers and ratings have the discharge books already described but, in addition, officers are also reported upon directly to their shipping company in the form of a Master's report. These reports are usually completed at six-monthly intervals or when an officer leaves a ship.

The reports used by some companies serve no useful purpose for they only ask for the barest of details and the word "Satisfactory" or "Average" against each item is accepted by the company. Other shipping companies, however, use comprehensive report forms modelled on the well-tried Naval pattern which call for full details on every aspect of the officer's personality and competence. While the Master is responsible for completing these reports he should draw on the advice of his heads of departments when reporting on individual officers.

Two important points arise from these Masters' reports. The first is that it is desirable for each report, whether it be good or bad, to be shown to the officer concerned; he should be required to sign it as evidence that he has read it. The second point is that the remarks shown in the Master's report should be in agreement with the comments given by that same Master in the officer's discharge book. No useful purpose—indeed, a great deal of harm—is served by a Master giving an officer a V.G. report in his discharge book and then reporting adversely on that officer's

behaviour or competence in his report to the shipowners. There
have been cases of shipping companies being prevented from
sacking an officer, reported by the Master (in his report) as being
incompetent or drunken, because the officer in question had a
Very Good report from the same Master in his official discharge
book.

(5) Warnings and discharge from the
Merchant Navy Establishment Scheme

The Merchant Navy Establishment Scheme is described elsewhere in this book.

All seamen, whether established or not, are subjected to the
same disciplinary procedures from the Administration of this
scheme.

Every seaman who is alleged to have committed an offence
is reported to the Administration and is interviewed by a local
committee. In smaller ports this committee may consist of the
local Administration officer and the local official of the seaman's
union. In larger ports, the committee consists of a shipping
company official, a representative of the British Shipping Federation and the branch secretary of the seaman's union. The
committee investigates the case and provided the members of the
committee are unanimous, the Chief Office of the Administration
confirms their findings and reprimand. If the members are not
unanimous, the case goes before the Central Committee on which
are high ranking officials from all sides of the industry.

The various degrees of reprimand were "warning", "severe
warning", "final warning" and, finally, "discharge". Recently
these have been altered to "caution", "suspension" and "ter-
mination of contract". If an established seaman receives one of
the warnings, he loses his establishment benefit but he may still
seek employment at sea; the unestablished seaman suffers no
financial loss at all. However, if an established seaman is "discharged" he is, in effect, expelled from the Merchant Navy
and must seek employment in some other industry.

An unestablished seaman who is "discharged" is likewise forced to seek employment in some other industry and, if this "discharge" arose from his refusal to join a particular ship, then he may lose his national insurance benefits.

Officers who have doubts about the efficiency of the Establishment Disciplinary Committees may be interested to learn that in twelve months August 1965 to July 1966, 2396 cases were dealt with of which 55 included officers. In 1370 cases the men were given a warning or severe warning, in 708 cases a final warning, and in 318 cases the men concerned were discharged.

CHAPTER 7

Crew Welfare

WELFARE is not just a question of supplying recreation rooms and film shows; welfare covers all aspects of human life at sea.

Shipowners have a very special problem so far as the welfare of their seamen is concerned, for these men spend long periods away from their families and from normal social and recreational facilities ashore. Seamen not only work aboard a ship but, apart from brief spells in port, they have to spend all their leisure time aboard that same ship. A ship's crew forms a small, isolated community and, if these men are to work efficiently as a team, the greatest attention should be paid to all the human factors affecting their well-being.

A shipowner may ask why he should have to provide special facilities for his crews and an officer may ask why he should make any special effort to secure the comfort and happiness of his men. The answer to both is that happiness breeds efficiency. If morale is high and the men are happy, then they will work more efficiently; they will accept changes and they will co-operate more readily with their officers and with shore management. A contented group of men are easier to control than a group who are dissatisfied with the conditions under which they are working. When the crew hate the ship in which they are serving there are incessant complaints about the food, there is wastage or destruction of equipment or stores, and problems of indiscipline arise.

Practically every man concerned with the operation of a ship has a part to play in improving the working and living conditions on board. The shipowner is the one, of course, who has the power to provide certain facilities, but his managers and superintendents need to take a sincere interest in the welfare of the men who man the ships; the Master and officers need to do all they can to establish good human relations on board; and the ratings need to respond whole-heartedly to the welfare facilities and activities provided for them. It is only by the joint effort of all concerned that conditions at sea can be brought up to the standard which all desire. Seamen are prone to blame their shipowners for poor conditions at sea—they need to realize that part of the blame lies with themselves.

Conditions at sea today are vastly superior to what they were fifty or a hundred years ago. Some people would argue that the improvement in conditions has been forced on the shipowners through sheer economic necessity; that shipowners have not really wanted to improve conditions but have done so simply to get enough men to man their ships. This may be partly true and we can use as evidence the fact that it is in the tanker companies (who find it difficult to get crews) where improvements are first introduced. The tanker companies were among the first to introduce swimming pools, single berth cabins and film shows into their ships and, now that the rest of the Merchant Navy has followed suit, these companies will have to look for further improvements in order to attract men to their ships. This is all to the good for everyone at sea has benefited from the lead set by these companies.

However, material comforts are not everything and some of the richer companies may have failed in their attempts to attract the men they want by attaching too much importance to material comforts and by not paying enough attention to the human side of their employment problem. Most seamen will agree that the happiest ships are not always the most modern and best-equipped ships; the happiest ships are the ones in which seamen feel that a genuine interest is being taken in their welfare and where they feel that they are recognized as people. The human side is far more important than the material side.

The whole subject of crew welfare is so vast that it will be divided into three sections—welfare facilities which can be provided by the shipowner for all his sea-going employees, recreational facilities which can be provided on board ship, and finally, activities on board which call for the involvement of the whole ship's company.

Welfare facilities

The most important step a shipowner can take is to set up a Welfare Department ashore under a high-ranking manager or superintendent. Some companies already have such departments and are finding that they are paying handsome dividends in building up a spirit of co-operation and security throughout their fleets.

The Welfare Department should deal with all human, domestic and personal problems which may arise. This department needs to have the power to act rapidly when domestic crises arise. For example, the department needs to be able to fly a man home to the sick-bed of a near relative without having to go through some lengthy procedure of getting financial permission from some other department. The Welfare Department needs to keep in touch with all the men at sea and with their wives and parents ashore; the names and telephone numbers of the people in the Welfare Department should be made known to all near relatives of the men at sea so that a wife can, if necessary, telephone a particular person if she suddenly finds herself in some difficulty. This information (on whom to telephone) can be posted to each wife directly by the company or sent by means of a printed, stamped, post-card given to each man as soon as he joins a ship.

The Welfare Department should keep a wife fully informed on her husband's movements and on the expected date of his next leave. If, for any reason, a man's leave is delayed, or if he is to be asked to join a ship before the end of his leave, his wife should be the first one to be told of the change in plan. A case can be made for the Welfare Department having, amongst its team, a woman "visitor" who could call on the wives of men away at sea and deal with any problems which may have arisen. Shipowners should take wives fully into their confidence and make them feel that they are just as important to the company as their seamen husbands.

At this point, it is worth commenting on the harm that is done by shipping companies who ask their officers to "help out" by joining ships before the end of their leaves. One of the main purposes in life for womenfolk is to rear children and it is here that their loyalty lies. Men have to provide for their families, with the result that they have two loyalties; one to their employers and one to their families. When a man is at sea, his wife probably accepts (reluctantly) that his loyalty and interest lie in the ship but, when he comes home on leave, his wife rightly expects her husband's interest and loyalty for the whole of that time. If, during the course of his leave, the company asks the man to "help out" by joining a ship long before the end of his leave period, the poor man is torn between loyalty to his wife and loyalty to his company. If, as usually happens, the man joins the ship as requested, his wife resents the company's interference with a period that was rightly hers. If this happens too often, she may persuade her husband to leave that company.

Shipowners who keep their ships running with men "helping out" are not running their ships efficiently. In "asking" men to return to ships before the end of their leaves, the company is abusing its power; men fear that they will incur the displeasure of their superiors if they refuse to help out too often.

There are, of course, occasions when a man, due to sail in a ship, suddenly falls ill or is needed at home to deal with some family crisis. In this case the company has to get a man on leave to take his place. These emergencies are accepted by loyal officers and their wives, particularly if the full details are explained to the man and his wife. What men resent are the brief telegrams received leave after leave asking them to return before the expiry of their leaves. They look upon this as mismanagement of personnel on the part of the company and rightly resent the curtailment of their leaves caused by the inability of their company to recruit and retain the right number of men.

Apart from dealing with domestic crises and explaining away

the curtailment of leaves, the Welfare Department can do a great deal of constructive work in drawing wives together, in inviting both wives and sea staff to the company's social functions at home, in arranging for the sea staff to visit places of interest in ports abroad, and in ensuring that sea staff are invited to social functions abroad.

Another important function of the Welfare Department would be to arrange for young officers and cadets to take part of their leaves abroad. This may prove to be impracticable for certificated officers who are needed to man the ship, but younger officers who request to take part of their leaves abroad should be encouraged to do so. Most seamen will agree that the "best" ports are not those with the brightest lights but those in which they have friends. By taking leaves in or near ports abroad served by his ship, a young officer will be enabled to establish friendships which could last him for the rest of his sea-going days. It should also be remembered that young men go to sea to see the world and they do not see it from the deck of a ship which only spends a few hours in port. The arrangements of taking leaves abroad may cause extra work for the Welfare Department, but this idea is worth pursuing by companies who want to give their men as full a life as possible and keep them at sea.

The forwarding of mail

A welfare facility which stands high in most seamen's list of priorities is the forwarding of mail from the United Kingdom to ships abroad. Some companies do this already, but many companies will not forward mail; instead they expect the seamen to keep their relatives and friends informed of their future addresses. This may be acceptable in ships on regular trades but it is a source of annoyance and discontent on tramp and other ships which frequently have changes in their destinations. The cost of forwarding mail by air lies between 1/- and 2/6 per man per week and a shipowner will have to decide whether an improvement in crew morale is worth this extra expense.

Carriage of wives

For many years now, some shipping companies have allowed
certain of their officers to carry their wives for one or more voyages
per year. Not all wives can take advantage of this facility for
some have young children who need to be cared for while others
are soon bored by the long ocean passages. Most newly-weds
welcome the chance of being together until the first child arrives,
and provided bathing and toilet facilities are adequate, there is
no reason why all officers should not be allowed to carry their wives.

At the same time, if officers are allowed to carry their wives,
there is no human reason for withholding this same facility from
company service ratings. In many ships, the ratings' accommodation is not suitable for the carriage of wives, but in one or two
new ships, facilities are being provided for the carriage of
ratings' wives.

There is the shipowner's point to view to be considered. Is it
quite fair to expect him to carry, care for, and feed the wives of
some or all of his crew-members? In fact, the life-boat accommodation and life-saving provisions may prevent him from doing
so even if he so wished. Thought could be given to the provision
of a certain amount of married accommodation aboard each new
ship and the number of wives restricted to the amount of married
accommodation available. Everyone who has sailed with a number of wives in one ship will know that the biggest problem is
related to the bathing and toilet facilities. This means that
married accommodation will have to consist of a number of
cabins each with its own day-room, bedroom and bathroom. The
provision of these suites will increase the cost of a ship and the
shipowner should be allowed to recover some of this cost by
making a charge for the occupation of this special accommodation.

Ship visiting

In some shipping companies today, officers and ratings have
to go through a somewhat degrading procedure in order to obtain

permission for their wives, fiancées and friends to visit their ships, while in other companies relatives and friends have almost free access to the ships.

Some shipowners say that they may leave themselves open to high liability claims if they opened their ships to the public and their view is supported by various dock, police and customs authorities in this country. These authorities tend to look on ship visitors as potential thieves, smugglers or immoral business people. While certain undesirable persons may board ships thrown open to the public, the most careful thought needs to be given to making ship visiting easier for friends and relatives of the crew and for members of the public who are genuinely interested in ships. In the long run, shipowners themselves will benefit from opening their ships to the public for parents will then see the fine conditions on ships, they will see seamen at work, and they will, possibly, encourage their own sons to go to sea. As things are today in Britain, members of the public do not know what conditions aboard ship are really like and they only see seamen ashore at play.

In Australia, New Zealand and South Africa and in many other countries, the docks are open to the public. Shore people enjoy visiting ships and the seamen derive a great deal of pleasure and pride from showing people around their ships. The seamen establish contacts with people who come from outside the usual dock environments and places of entertainment and they strike up friendships which, in some cases, last for many years. In the countries where the docks are open to the public, seamen are much more integrated with society ashore than they are in Britain. The closed dock system of Britain helps to confirm the seamen's belief that he does not belong to normal shore society and that he comes from a race apart; he then behaves accordingly.

Shipowners need to look very carefully at their own views on ship visiting and should relax all control of this aspect as much as possible. Shipowners should give very clear instructions to their Masters on the question of ship visiting.

In order to protect themselves from claims for personal injuries sustained while on board, shipping companies should insist on each visitor signing an indemnity form before he boards the ship. This system is already in operation in some companies and is found to work reasonably well.

ESTABLISHING CONTACT BETWEEN OFFICERS AND SHIPPERS. People ashore in Britain love ships, and seamen are proud of their work. Some shipowners have already seen the benefits which come from encouraging their Chief Officers to visit the factories of their more important shippers. The shipper is pleased to talk, at first hand, to the man who looks after his cargo at sea and the ship's officer is proud to be recognized as a man who has a very important role to play in the exporting efforts of this country. Mutual goodwill and understanding is established on both sides and, quite often, a visit from a ship's officer results in increased shipments from the shipper.

All the points mentioned so far call for policy decisions on the part of shipowners; there is very little a ships' officer can do to introduce any of the schemes described above.

The shipowner also has the major role to play in building or fitting out his ship in a certain way and in supplying certain items of equipment. These items are dealt with briefly below.

Accommodation

Crew accommodation is already controlled by the Crew Accommodation Regulations and, in most ships today, the accommodation provided is adequate. Furnishings, which are not covered by the Regulations, are not always adequate and the most careful thought needs to be given to supplying ratings with comfortable chairs or settees and to supplying table covers in their dining saloons.

It is the duty of the Master to see that the accommodation is kept clean. In some ships the Master carries out a daily inspection of the ship while in most cargo ships the only inspection carried out is on the Master's routine Sunday morning "rounds". It has been suggested that Masters should make spot checks during the week to make sure that the accommodation is kept n the condition in which it was during the previous Sunday's rounds.

Food

Some people claim that food is the most important factor in determining the happiness or contentment of a crew and they may well be right. Seamen look on food as part of their remuneration and, on a long ocean passage with little else to talk about, their thoughts gravitate towards the food they are being given. It should be remembered, too, that when a ship is at sea, the crew cannot supplement their diets in any way; they are wholly dependent on the food issued to them.

Many companies appreciate the importance of good food served in an attractive manner and they give every encouragement to their Chief Stewards to provide attractive and varied menus.

However, because food costs can be precisely determined, this part of the ship's running costs often catches the eye of the company's accountants with the result that the Chief Steward is over-controlled from the shore and is continually urged to reduce these feeding costs. If only food costs were not so easily determined (as are some of the other costs aboard ships) there would probably be less control from the shore. Some shipowners need to re-examine their control of Chief Stewards and to encourage them to use their own initiative in the purchasing of foodstuffs abroad. More use should be made of the excellent document prepared by the Liverpool Nautical Catering College. This document lists all the foodstuffs available at most of the major ports abroad and shows when the various items are at their best or cheapest.

The cooking and serving of food is one of the most thankless tasks aboard a ship and everyone aboard should co-operate with the Chief Steward and cooks in making their task easier. Seamen should be just as ready to congratulate the steward on an excellent meal as they are to complain about a bad meal. Any complaints about food should be as precise as possible so that the steward or cook can understand exactly what was unacceptable to the crew and take steps to remedy the defects.

Recreational facilities

Recreation rooms

Most ships today are fitted with a crew's recreation room but, in many ships, these rooms are so badly furnished and equipped that they are rarely used. Some shipowners may wonder, when they see that the recreation rooms are not being used, why they bothered fitting them. The answer may lie in shipowners re-designing their recreational rooms and providing one, comfortably furnished, quiet room and one games/hobbies room for noisier activities.

It has been suggested, recently, that there should be one recreational or community centre for the whole of the ship's company. These community centres may be ideal in ships of the future (manned by five men plus a psychiatrist to keep them happy!) but may not be acceptable at present.

Officers' and crew's bars

If the crew are to be expected to work together as a team, they should see their officers living and working together as a team. The most positive way in which a shipowner can introduce a team concept into his ships is by fitting an officers' bar or ward-room and by stopping drinking in cabins. Then, too, if the officers have a bar, the crew should also be given a bar.

Crew bars have been fitted in passenger ships for many years and, generally, they have been successful. It is only in recent years that cargo ships have been fitted with crew's bars and, from all reports received, these too are working well.

There are a number of problems connected with bars aboard

ship and a shipowner needs to consider all these problems and needs to issue a clear policy statement to his Masters before introducing bars into his ships.

Most ships have the space for a bar in the officers' smokeroom and in the crew's recreation room. The main problem concerns staffing the bars. In some ships a steward is appointed as barman for the officers' bar while in other ships the officers take turns in acting as barman; the former method is the more preferable of the two for, as so often happens with the willing horse getting the major share of the work, one officer may find that he is expected to do more than his fair share of bar keeping.

Bar hours are another problem for, even if a steward is appointed, this steward cannot be expected to work all hours. Many ships open the bar from 1200 to 1300 and again from 1700 to 2100. We must then decide what ought to be done about making liquor available to officers outside these hours. One way is to allow officers to purchase bottled drinks from the bar during normal opening hours but, then, this may encourage certain officers to revert to their traditional habits of drinking in their cabins with a few selected friends. A preferable method of making drinks available outside normal hours is to leave the bar open and ask each officer to sign for any drinks consumed. The bar may suffer some losses under this system and these losses will have to be shared equally amongst all the officers.

Prices and methods of payments cause more problems. In some ships, all drinks are sold at cost price; in other ships, a surcharge is placed on all drinks to recover part of the wages and overtime payments for the appointed barman, while in still other ships, the officers voluntarily pay a surcharge in order to build up a mess fund for the purchase of tape-recorders, records, and other equipment, and to pay for the joint entertainment of visitors to the ship.

In a few ships all drinks are paid for in cash but, in most ships, the officers sign chits for all drinks consumed. This latter method is preferable for many reasons, one of which is that the Master can effect some sort of control over anyone who drinks to excess.

Most ships' bars enforce a non-treating rule and, in the long run, this is better than allowing treating. Unfortunately this prevents the playing of liar dice and other games for rounds of drinks and many Masters relax the non-treating rule when these games are played in the bar.

Bars can be put to good use in bringing the officers together and in relieving part of the load on the stewards. One idea which has been tried with some success is the serving of "pub" lunches in the bar each Saturday. The stewards prepare a buffet type lunch and simply leave it in the bar for the officers to help themselves. This gives the Cook some relief from his daily tasks and relieves the Saloon Steward for at least one meal during the week. The cooks and stewards on the ships which have adopted this idea have welcomed it. The only problem which arises comes from the one officer who insists on having a cooked lunch at mid-day!

Crew's bars are just as important as officers' bars. When the crew bar is properly organized and managed it can prove to be a tremendous asset to a ship. One of the advantages arises in port when, instead of the crew going ashore at mid-day for a drink and then forgetting to return until the following morning, they can go to their own bar for a beer or two and then resume their normal work after lunch.

In passenger ships, appointed personnel serve in the crew's bar but in cargo ships men are just not available for bar duty. This problem is overcome in some ships by allowing one of the petty officers to draw bar stock from the Chief Steward and then to sell it to the rest of the crew at whatever price is decided upon. Most crews voluntarily pay a surcharge on their drinks in order to build up a social fund. In some ships this fund is used to buy extra equipment for the bar, any balance going towards a party at the end of the voyage. In other ships the crew use the fund to hire coaches at ports abroad in order to visit places of interest, the most ambitious venture being the hiring of an aeroplane by one crew in an Australian port in order to visit Canberra! In some ships, the crew fund has been invested in various companies ashore. This can only be done in ships on regular trades which have the same crew for voyage after voyage and then problems arise when one man wishes to withdraw his stake in the fund.

One of the problems which has arisen in connection with crew bars concerns the type of alcohol which should be served. Some companies insist on nothing stronger than beer being made available in the crew bar while other companies allow beer and spirits to be served. While companies should lay down broad policies on this question, the Master of a ship should have some freedom to allow certain types of alcohol to be served in the bars aboard his ship. A Master may find it advantageous to commence the voyage with beer only in the crew bar and then to make spirits available once it has been determined that the bar facilities are not being abused; the Master will be able to get some factual advice from his Petty Officers on this subject. It has been found in most ships operating bars that both officers and ratings have responded very favourably to the bar facilities provided.

Hobbies room

While some seamen still follow hobbies, widespread interest in hobbies has declined both ashore and at sea. The hobbies which can be followed at sea, and the equipment needed for each, are described in the excellent book *Spare Time at Sea*[5], now, unfortunately, out of print. Some shipowners have provided well-equipped hobbies rooms in ships, but the use of these rooms is by no means uniform in the ships so equipped. Shipowners must find it difficult to decide on just what equipment and tools should be provided and will look on the cost of equipment supplied as a waste of money if it is not properly used.

Men who are keen photographers or model makers usually carry their own equipment. Why, then, provide hobbies rooms? Is the intention to stimulate seamen into taking up new hobbies as a result of which they may become more contented at sea? While the answer to the second question may be in the affirmative, seamen can use hobby rooms to their advantage.

Each one of us has various needs and urges, some of which are: (a) the need to earn a living, (b) the need to keep physically fit, (c) the need for social contact with others, and (d) the need to engage in some sort of creative activity. Each person is able, with varying degrees of success, to satisfy these needs (a), above, by being trained for a particular job, (b) by engaging in physical recreation, and (c) by meeting people and making friends. The man ashore satisfies (d), above, by digging in his garden, decorating his house, putting up shelves, or messing about with his motor car. These activities are simply not available to the man at sea, so how, then, can he find some form of creative activity? To answer this question we must cast around for some creative activities which can be carried out aboard ship. There must be many suitable activities, but two suggestions may help seamen to move along satisfying paths.

The first concerns teaching models. Most seamen will have passed through some sort of training establishment and they will be aware that some of these schools lack working models of parts of ships. Seamen may like to explore the idea of making working models of derricks, hatch-covers, pumps, steering gears, winches, engines, etc., and then selling them to nautical training establishments. They may be able to cut through condemned cargo-blocks, shackles, and items of machinery, polish up and paint the exposed parts and make valuable teaching items for schools. They will probably find that a ready market exists for really good teaching aids not only in nautical establishments, but also in ordinary schools both in Britain and abroad. More ambitious projects would be the manufacture of scale models of parts of the ship—the focs'le head, the fore-peak, a cross-section through a hold, the stern section. Model stern tubes could be made. The list of teaching aids which can be made aboard ship is almost endless.

The second concerns toys. Many seamen already make toys for their own children, but more seamen may like to consider making toys for children's homes. Provided the toys are safe, strong and child-proof, they will always be accepted with gratitude by the people running these homes.

Some seamen make furniture, others make boats. These and many other items can all be made in the well-equipped hobby room and a seaman who becomes absorbed in some worthwhile hobby will find that time at sea passes very quickly.

Libraries

Without doubt, the most welcome welfare facility at sea are the ships' libraries supplied by the Seafarers' Education Service. All praise is due to the S.E.S. for the sterling work they do in keeping ships supplied with books; they rightly enjoy the gratitude of practically every man in the Merchant Navy. Those shipowners who do not subscribe to the S.E.S. library scheme may find it to their advantage to re-examine their ideas on the importance of ships' libraries.

The usual ship's library consists of a mixture of fiction and non-fictional books but, in addition to these books, ships require a permanent reference library. Some shipowners are already supplying their ships with permanent reference books many of which appear to be connected with their cadets' study courses. It could be said that more thought needs to be given to supplying ships with the right reference books. How many ships for example carry the International Labour Office book *Safety in Dock Work*[8] and the *Chain Testers' Handbook*[1]? Yet these books are invaluable sources of information to all officers concerned with the carriage of cargo. Officers also need good reference books on corrosion and painting, on marine engines, on electricity and electronics, and on the preparation and cooking of various dishes.

A shipowner may well ask where he is going to stow these reference books, which are only used occasionally. The answer may lie in supplying the ships with micro-feische readers and supplying the reference books on micro-film. These micro-readers are not expensive (about £38) and they would also be of great use to cadets and others following correspondence courses. One of the problems associated with studying by correspondence at sea is that each course must, of necessity, be geared to one or two textbooks. If only ships were fitted with micro-readers, shore tutors could use a wide range of textbooks and micro-filmed extracts could be posted to students by airmail.

Magazines

Once they have obtained their certificates, some officers cease to take any further interest in modern developments in shipping. It is the duty of every officer to keep up to date, and he can best do this by reading up-to-date magazines. There are many technical magazines published which contain material of interest to the ships' officer and rating, the *Shipping World and Shipbuilder*, the *Shipbuilding and Shipping Record*, the *Motor Ship*, the *Nautical Magazine*, the *Dock and Harbour Authority*, and the *Fairplay International Shipping Journal* are some of the titles which come to mind. Possibly the most important journals are *Safety at Sea International* which contains information on all aspects of safety at sea and the *Journal of Commerce Annual Review* which contains information on all modern developments which are taking place in the shipping industry.

Some shipowners supply some of these magazines to their ships but the majority of shipowners supply no magazines whatsoever. Should shipowners supply magazines or should ships' officers take out personal subscriptions for the magazines of their choice? On balance, it seems preferable for officers to take out their own subscriptions for they can then be sure of getting the magazines they want. It is an unfortunate fact that magazines sent to some Masters for distribution throughout the ship are left in a pile under the Master's settee and are only distributed when long out of date. If seamen are to be encouraged to take out personal subscriptions to magazines then their shipowners will need to make some provision for forwarding these magazines to the men concerned; publishing houses would not take kindly to sending each issue to a different agent's address abroad.

Airmail editions of major British newspapers have been available for many years now and some seamen take advantage of this service. This certainly keeps these men in closer touch with home and world affairs than those men who do not read a newspaper during the whole of a voyage.

Shipowners may like to consider sending copies of daily and Sunday newspapers to their ships, but a better method may be for shipowners to subscribe to a radio news service so that daily news reports may be obtained on board their cargo ships as is already done on passenger ships. This will, unfortunately, put an extra work load on the ship's radio officer.

Once weather facsimile recorders are widely used at sea, the problems of ships' newspapers may be overcome. The Japanese are already sending the front page of a daily newspaper at the end of each main weather transmission and there is no reason why the British transmitting stations should not do the same.

Ship's broadcasting system

While many ships today are fitted with a ship's radio and broadcasting system, the fact that most seamen have their personal transistor radio sets means that the ship's broadcasting system is not always used to full advantage. In some ships the broadcasting system is used more for the transmission of recorded music than for the broadcasting of radio programmes. Continuous music has a soothing effect on any group of people working under stress; that is why it is so widely used in factories ashore. On ships, however, most of the crew are employed out on deck, in noisy machinery spaces or in remote parts of the ship so that the supply of continuous music is not a practical proposition.

Some companies are equipping their ships with tape recorders and gramophones and are supplying recorded music. To date, this practice is not as widespread in cargo ships as it is in passenger ships.

Film service

A very popular welfare service is film shows. Ships carry their own projectors and obtain films from depots in major ports throughout the world.

Although this service is rather expensive, it does do a lot of good in improving morale on board by creating interest in things outside the ship, thus enabling seafarers to escape, for a short period, from the narrow confines of their ship. The provision of film shows on cargo ships is becoming more widespread and most seamen are coming to expect this service.

One of the problems which arises from film shows is in trying to decide who should operate the projector. In some ships, one of the junior officers is expected to do this work outside his normal hours of duty, while in other ships the job of film projectionist is given to the ship's electrician. One solution to this problem may be to train a rating to operate the projector and then to pay him overtime for all the time he spends on carrying out this task outside his normal working hours.

Television sets

Some passenger ships are permanently fitted with television sets while others pick them up on first arrival in port. On cargo ships, no uniform practice exists for the provision of television sets on board. Some of the more progressive companies have arrangements with rental firms under which television sets are supplied to their ships while in United Kingdom ports, the rental charges being met by the shipping companies.

In other companies, however, the officers and crews have to buy or hire their own television sets. This does not always work satisfactorily for, if a man has paid his share of the cost of the set and is then relieved suddenly before the ship sails, he finds it difficult to recover his share of the cost. Shipping companies should try to supply television sets at no charge to the individuals in the ship.

Modern cultural, educational and entertainment devices

Suggestions have been made that ships could be equipped with slide projectors, loop projectors, language machines, teaching machines and video tape-recorders. All these items are good and could be used to stimulate interest aboard ship, but two—the video tape-recorder and the language machine—call for particular mention.

Although the video tape-recorder can be used for entertainment purposes, its main use lies in improving efficiency aboard ships.

The machinery of modern ships is becoming more and more complicated. It is common practice, when a new ship is being built, for the first Chief and Second Engineers to be sent to the engine-builder's factory to see the machinery being made and, subsequently, fitted in the ship. These engineers become very familiar with this machinery yet, when they are eventually sent on leave, they are expected to hand over all the details and problems associated with the machinery to their reliefs in a matter of a few hours. The poor relief engineers then have to turn to the instructional manuals whenever a repair or maintenance job has to be done. If only ships were supplied with video tape-recorders, the installation of the engines could be filmed and left on tape in the ship. Repair jobs which necessitated the opening up of parts of the machinery could likewise be filmed and left on tape in the ship. If, later in the ship's life, similar repair or maintenance work had to be carried out, the serving Chief and Second Engineers could play back the relevant tapes and plan their work programme in the light of any snags they notice on the televised films.

The Master and Deck Officers could also make use of video tape-recorders. If a particular company started using a new port, the first ship entering that port could film the approaches, the berths and the cargo handling facilities. Copies of this tape could then be sent to the rest of the ships in the fleet and Masters of subsequent ships entering that port could play the tape and plan their approach courses and berthing procedures in advance. It may be asked why video tape-recorders should be used in preference to traditional film cameras and projectors. The answer lies in the facts that the video tape requires no processing and that tapes can be played back on a simple television set thus removing the need to erect a screen and projector in a darkened room, as is required in the case of normal film shows. Unfortunately the cost of video tape-recorders and cameras is still very high and a good set would cost between £500 and £1000.

The language machine is, however, a cheap and very effective item of equipment. A machine plus two languages can be obtained for under £200. The language machine is, essentially, a tape-recorder with provision made for listening to the native voice and recording the student's voice. A safety device is fitted so that the master track cannot be inadvertently erased. A keen student of average ability should be able to learn to speak a language reasonably well after 100 to 150 hours at the machine. When one compares this time with the length of a passage across the Pacific, it can be seen that a man could almost learn a language in one crossing. The advantage of learning a language on one of these machines stems from the privacy it affords; the student is not afraid to speak out loud when trying the various phrases. Also, on playing back the tape, the student can compare his own efforts with the native voice and can practise certain difficult phrases as many times as he likes.

Washing machines

Very few seamen actually enjoy washing their clothes yet this job has to be done. Some modern cargo ships are fitted with washing machines for both the officers and the crew but there are many ships at sea today which have none of these machines. Some shipowners claim that the machines are misused and that maintenance costs on them are too high. If, however, a shipowner wants his officers to be neatly dressed in white uniforms in the tropics then he is under some obligation to supply washing and drying facilities. Nothing is more disheartening to an officer than having to wash his clothes in the officers' bathroom and then having to hang them in his cabin to dry.

Sports and recreational items

In many ships, the only recreational equipment supplied by the shipowner are dartboards and table tennis sets. There are, however, many other items which can be introduced at no great cost to the shipowner—in fact, many of the items listed below could be made or bought by the ship's company.

The most glaring omission from ships is a piano, yet those few ships which do carry pianos find them of inestimable value as a focal point for some social gatherings in the evening. Second-hand pianos can be bought at a very low price in Britain, in fact many people are prepared to give away their old pianos provided the new owner pays the removal expenses. People interested in the welfare of ships' crews may like to explore the possibility of supplying ships with old pianos. The siting of pianos aboard ship is important for, if they are too close to sleeping accommodation, they will cause annoyance to watchkeepers who may be trying to sleep while the rest of the ship's company is singing at the piano.

Most passenger ships have part of their decks marked out with courts for deck tennis, deck golf and deck quoits. These games are very popular with passengers and could prove to be equally as popular with the crews of cargo ships. Some cargo ships already have these courts marked out, but many more ships could lay out their decks for these games. Great care must be taken in the siting of these courts and they should never be above sleeping accommodation; nothing is more irritating to a man trying to get to sleep than the thump of quoits on the deck above.

Some ships have experimented with the floodlighting of empty holds for the playing of badminton. This is a step in the right direction for one of the problems at sea which has so far defied solution is the problem of physical recreation on board ship. The traditional deck games do not appeal to everyone at sea and proficiency in these games does not necessarily enable a seafarer to enter into sporting activities ashore. The solution to the problem of physical recreation at sea may lie in equipping ships with gymnasia, squash courts and sailing dinghies, all of which are expensive and heavy. There must be simpler solutions to this problem and there does seem to be a great need for someone to devote a lot of effort and thought to the invention of a new game which will appeal to the majority of sailors. The game should, so far as possible, be similar to one played ashore so that a seaman, by playing this game regularly at sea, will become proficient in this particular sport and will, thus, be able to join in the activities of a sports club ashore while on leave or when his ship is in port. On one or two ships, officers have built their own golfing machines. These usually consist of a tee and a bit of canvas marked with a bull's eye. More sophisticated machines can be purchased in Japan and elsewhere. These consist of an electronically controlled screen which indicates whether or not the ball has been properly struck and how far it has travelled. A seaman searching for a creative hobby may like to develop or modify a shore game so it can be played aboard ship; he would probably find a ready market for his invention in other ships. Someone may even like to think about developing magnetic billiards or table football for use aboard ship.

In order to assist seamen draw up their own sports courts, the sizes are given below:

DECK TENNIS. The court should be about 30 feet long and about 13 feet wide. On each side of the net there should be a neutral space 3 feet wide and parallel to this neutral line, and about 6 feet from each end of the court, should be the back line. A fore-and-aft line should be drawn along the midlength of the court between the back and the neutral lines as shown in Fig. 7.1. The net should be at shoulder height. The rules and scoring are as for tennis except that no player may put his foot in the neutral space.

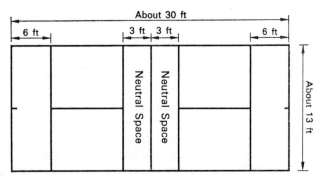

FIG. 7.1. Layout of a deck tennis court. "Tramlines" may be drawn down each side to convert the singles court into a doubles court.

DECK QUOITS. The court should consist of two sets of concentric circles, about 29 feet apart, centre to centre as illustrated in Fig. 7.2. Each set consists of three concentric circles, the centre circle being of 6 inches radius (score 3 points), the next being 15 inches radius (score 2 points), and the largest being 24 inches radius (score 1 point). Twelve inches in front of the largest circle, and running athwart the line of the course, is the dead (or ladies') line. Twelve inches behind the largest circle and running parallel to the dead line is the serving line. The rules are similar to those used for bowls ashore.

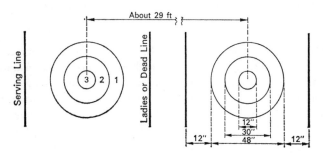

FIG. 7.2. Layout of a deck quoits court.

Activities on board

There are a number of activities which can be held aboard ship and which call for the active participation of some or all the ship's company. The success of these activities is wholly dependent on the enthusiasm of the senior officers and petty officers.

Sports committees

The first step is to set up a sports committee of representatives from all sections of the ship's company. The chairman may be the Master, one of the officers or one of the ratings. This committee should draw up sports and recreational programmes which should reflect the interest of most of the ship's company; it need hardly be said that it is a waste of time introducing a certain activity if no-one supports it. It has been found, in many ships, that these sports committees help to bridge the gulf between officers and crew. Sporting activities do bring men closer together and officers should look on it as their duty to participate in as many activities as possible. No officer should hesitate to play any game with or against a rating; in fact an officer's intrinsic status will grow, the more he participates in the sporting activities on board the ship.

Team sports

Many ships have football and cricket teams and morale in these ships is usually very high; all hands feel they are joined together in a common venture when their ship's team plays against another ship. Local officials of the Missions to Seamen are only too willing to arrange games between ships.

Often, however, team sports in port create problems for the Chief Officer or Second Engineer who may require the men to carry out maintenance work; it is up to the officer concerned to work out his own order of priorities. Work which is essential to the efficient and safe operation of the ships should be carried out but less essential work could possibly be sacrificed for an improvement in crew morale.

Sports afternoons

One way of increasing enthusiasm for deck sports in a ship is to hold a sports tournament in which each department on board puts forward participants for each game and where each winner gains points for his department.

Owing to the seaman's habit of resting in the afternoon, these games should not commence before 1600 and, in order to overcome the problem of mealtimes and to free the catering department for participation in the tournament, a buffet supper and beer should be arranged out on deck.

Special evenings

Another way of breaking the monotony of a long ocean passage is to arrange one or more "special" evenings. These may take the form of special dinners for the officers or ratings or they may be combined functions to be attended by men from both sections of the ship. Provided the weather is suitable, part of one of the decks can be decorated and drinks and a buffet meal served. In one particular ship, "cowboy" nights were held; the deck was decorated as a western saloon and all hands were invited to attend in clothes of that era.

Choirs and musical groups

In one or two ships, members of the crew have come together spontaneously and have formed choirs and guitar groups. This is an activity which must be spontaneous for no amount of coaxing will force men to sing or perform well. If, however, it is noticed that a group has formed, the Master or senior officers should give this group every encouragement. One way of giving this encouragement is by persuading the men to perfect a number of items and then arranging for them to play in clubs or pubs in ports visited by the ship. In one particular ship, trading between Australia and America, the choir was so good that they had a large following in the ports visited. As a result of their musical accomplishments, the crew of this ship were welcomed in ports abroad and struck up many long lasting friendships; they also found that they did not have to pay for many drinks ashore!

Gambling on board

The card games played on board ship for money or cigarettes are well known and, for the most part, the stakes are not very high. Some people are against gambling on moral grounds and we must respect their views. There are, however, a number of games which can be used to bring the ship's company closer together.

Some ships hold football pools in which each man taking part is given a League football team, the prize going to the man whose team scores exactly 11 goals. This creates some interest in the weekly football results but it also creates extra work for the Master who has to make up the accounts of wages and for the radio officer who has to get the football results. This particular game does not really bring men closer together and may not be worth the effort which goes into its organization.

An evening's racing certainly brings men together. The usual way in which this game is played is for horses to be moved along a prepared course on the throw of a dice. Six horses and two dice are used. The first dice thrown indicates the number of the horse and the second dice gives the number of places it is to move. The horses may be "bought" and the owner of the winning horse takes a percentage of all the stake money on that race. One of the problems which prevents the wider use of this type of racing aboard cargo ships is that the crew do not have cash, and to hold an evening's racing on a chit system would cause too much work for the Master or Purser. One way of overcoming this problem is for the ship to carry a supply of small change and those wishing to take part in the racing evening could draw some of this money against their wages.

Still another game which brings men closer together is bingo or housey-housey. Once again there is the problem of small change and it can be overcome as mentioned above.

On the "special evenings" mentioned earlier in this chapter, roulette wheels and other games have been used with success. All these games, however, call for a supply of small change which will have to be obtained by the Master or Purser at the start of the voyage.

Lectures and debates

In some ships very successful lecture and debating evenings have been held. The lectures may be given by officers or ratings and may be on any subject of interest, a very popular topic being the facilities in the next port to be visited by the ship. Material for such a lecture can be obtained from the Pilot Book for the area and from Dr. Hope's excellent book *A Shore-goer's Guide to World Ports*[6]. Personal experiences can also be used, but care must be taken to prevent the lecture degenerating into a discussion on the facilities and prices in dock-side pubs. An officer trying to introduce a lecture programme into a ship may find initial opposition but, if he perseveres, he will probably be surprised at the amount of interesting and knowledgeable information held by various members of the ship's company, especially by some of the ratings. Care must be taken to set the correct environment for the lecture. Once lecture evenings have become an established part of the ship's life, they could be used to advantage by officers charged with the training of cadets. The giving of a lecture does help build up self-confidence and each cadet could be instructed to deliver a lecture on any subject of his choice.

Debates have proved to be popular in some ships and much depends on the enthusiasm of the organizer and on the selection of interesting topics. The debate should be properly controlled if it is to be successful. A proposer and seconder should be nominated to support and oppose the motion and each should be limited in length of his address. After the main speeches, the motion should be thrown open to the floor for discussion and followed by a wind-up speech, by one man from each side, before a vote is taken. Care must be taken to prevent the open discussion degenerating into an argument between two persons on the floor.

The activities described above are only a few of the things which can be done aboard ship. The success of these activities depends on all the members of the ship's company. Experiments should be carried out in order to determine which activities appeal to the majority of the men aboard but, by the introduction of some of the activities described here, the morale of the ship can be improved; this has nothing to do with the shipowner.

Membership of clubs ashore

Some shipping companies have sports and social clubs in ports abroad for both their sea and shore staffs. Many officers derive a great deal of pleasure from membership of these clubs; it is a pity that seafarers are sometimes rejected by shore people because of the objectionable behaviour of one or two seafarers after they have consumed too much alcohol. It cannot be overstressed that men must be on their very best behaviour when in clubs ashore if these club facilities are not to be withdrawn from all seafarers.

CHAPTER 8

Shipboard Liaison Representatives

BEFORE examining the National Union of Seamen's Shipboard Liaison Scheme in detail, we should firstly look at the use of shop-stewards in industries ashore.

Freedom to associate with whom we like is one of our fundamental rights. Another of our rights is that any group of men is free to choose a spokesman to act on its behalf. In Britain today, there are thousands of shop-stewards some of whom do nothing more than collect subscriptions and issue ballot papers. The great majority of shop-stewards are happily integrated into the structure of their firms and unions and are accepted by employers as accredited union officials and as representatives of the men.

To a lot of workers, the shop-steward *is* the union. Through him they join the union, pay their subscriptions, have their complaints settled, and hear of new agreements. It is no wonder that some shop-stewards can command a loyal following when differences with their parent unions arise. Strikes actually called by shop-stewards in defiance of their unions are few and far between. This type of labour trouble may arise when, in a large factory employing men from a number of different unions, the shop-stewards form a joint committee. Sometimes the shop-stewards are more loyal to this committee than they are to their parent unions.

The functions of shop-stewards differ slightly between one union and another but, in general, they are:

(1) to encourage recruitment and interest in the organization of the union;

(2) to collect subscriptions and to inspect members' cards for arrears;

(3) to ensure the carrying out of existing agreements, practices, customs and habits; and

(4) to represent members' interests and to negotiate any dispute which may arise with foremen and management.

Owing to the unique situation at sea where, on board each ship, all hands must live and work together in a close-knit community in which it is essential that the system of authority is preserved, the duties and powers of liaison representatives are not the same as those of shop-stewards in shore industries. The shipboard liaison representative is *not* a shop-steward in the full meaning of the word. The liaison representative has no power to negotiate variations of matters already settled by the National Maritime Board and he has no power to represent a man in any dispute between that man and the Master.

The duties of Liaison Representatives are clearly laid down in the N.U.S. Shipboard Handbook[15]. These duties are:

(a) to keep members informed of industrial and union developments and to supply them with union publications;

(b) to advise members how to use the union's machinery and services and to assist in this direction;

(c) to ensure that all appropriate ratings are N.U.S. members financially in compliance by reporting any breaches to the union official or office as soon as possible;

(d) to encourage members to use the National Maritime Board Complaints Procedure when necessary, to advise members how to take up *bona fide* complaints (thus co-operating in the efficient operation of ships) and to report to the union and the Master all unresolved cases taken up under this procedure;

(e) to encourage members to study and otherwise take an interest in union and industrial subjects and, where required, to organize educational activities;

(f) to encourage and co-operate in social and welfare activities where special committees to do this are non-existent; and to keep the union informed of happenings on board ship outside the normal.

The regulations drawn up by the union make it quite clear:

(a) that liaison representatives are expected at all times to act in the best interests of the union and its members;

(b) that they are expected to co-operate with Masters and officers towards the efficient operation of the ship;

(c) that no industrial action may be taken or initiated by a liaison representative under any circumstances unless under specific instruction from the union's head office by its national officials;

(d) that no action must be taken or initiated which would prejudice the right of an individual seaman to make a complaint under the provisions of the Articles or the Merchant Shipping Acts;

(e) that liaison representatives, either individually or collectively, must not interfere or intervene in the affairs of any ship other than their own;

(f) that liaison representatives have no rights under the Complaints Procedure other than as individuals and, therefore, cannot accompany or represent members when taking up matters, other than at the express request of the Master or officer concerned and with the consent of the individual member/s involved;

(g) that it is no part of their duties to adjudicate on the interpretation of N.M.B. agreements; any questions of interpretation must be referred to the union through the appropriate full-time officials;

(h) that liaison representatives must carry out their duties outside their own working hours;

(i) that the activities of liaison representatives must be confined to members of the N.U.S.; and

(j) that any contravention of the union's regulations or any behaviour which is not within the spirit and intention of the scheme would make the liaison representative concerned liable to the refusal or withdrawal of union endorsement and/or penalties within the provisions of the union's rules.

The qualifications of liaison representatives are laid down in the *Shipboard Handbook*[15]. Each representative:

(a) must have at least five years' continuous union membership and five years' sea service;

(b) must be at least 23 years of age;

(c) must have a clear record of conduct for at least twelve months immediately prior to inclusion on the panel of accredited potential liaison representatives drawn up by the N.U.S.;

(d) must have taken or be willing to take one of the union's training courses; and

(e) must be prepared to signify acceptance of the conditions of appointment as laid down in the union's regulations.

The method of appointment of a liaison representative is straightforward and has been laid down in the *Shipboard Handbook*[15].

(a) Prior to the departure of a ship on a voyage, the district secretary of the National Union of Seamen will appoint a member of long standing and experience to act as convener and will notify the Master accordingly.

The convener will call a meeting or meetings of N.U.S. members aboard as soon as possible after, and in any case within seven days of sailing from the U.K. port concerned for the purpose of receiving nominations for the liaison representative or representatives and for making arrangements for any ballot necessary.

The appointment must be made by secret ballot and the convener will inform the Master and the union of the result of such election. The convener will be responsible for the conduct of any further election and may, if required, act as referee in any dispute among members arising from the implementation of the scheme.

(b) Union liaison representatives may be elected, by crew personnel who are members of the N.U.S., for the period covered by the Articles but in any case shall be subject to re-election at the end of six months.

(c) (i) In ships of up to 30 members there may be one liaison representative for all departments.

(ii) In ships with over 30 members there may be one representative for each of the three departments: deck, engine and catering.

(iii) Additionally, in larger ships where the number of members in a particular department exceeds 100, special arrangements may be made between the N.U.S. and the companies concerned to provide for additional liaison representatives.

(d) Where there are two or more candidates, all liaison representatives shall be elected by secret ballot vote at or following the special ship or departmental meetings. No election shall be valid unless at least two-thirds of the members eligible have voted. If less than two-thirds of such valid votes are cast, this will be taken to mean that no representatives will be elected for the ship or department concerned for the particular voyage or for six months, whichever is the shorter, unless the procedure set out in (g) below is observed.

(e) Nomination for liaison representatives shall be by crew members from those on board who are on the union's list of accredited potential representatives. The convener is not himself precluded from being nominated and elected provided his name is on that list.

(f) Where there are no members from the union's list available, however, the crew members concerned may elect a representative who has the necessary qualifications, subject to his endorsement by the union.

(g) If at least one-third of the eligible members of a department (or of a ship where there are less than 31 members) are dissatisfied with the conduct of their representative, or if they wish to elect a representative where none has been appointed under paragraph

(d) above, a departmental or ship meeting will be called by the convener to consider the matter. If the meeting decides to conduct a new election for a liaison representative it shall be done in accordance with these regulations.

(h) Elected liaison representatives (on ships of over 30 members) shall co-ordinate their activities and duties in order to carry out the principles of this scheme. To this end they may appoint, from among themselves, a co-ordinator or may call upon the convener to act in that capacity.

Any member of the National Union of Seamen has the right to appeal to the union if he feels dissatisfied with any aspect of the operation of the Liaison Scheme.

When the scheme was first introduced it was agreed by both the union and the shipowners that it would be tried out in a few selected ships and that only after teething troubles had been remedied would it be extended to other ships. The success of the experiments to date has allayed a number of fears about the scheme and it is now being extended to other ships.

The Pearson Report[20] recommended that, provided adequate safeguards are kept, the system of shipboard representation should be extended throughout the Merchant Navy as rapidly as possible. Lord Pearson went on to say that there should not be any major revision of the scheme, nor should there be any changes in the powers and duties of liaison representatives until sufficient time has elapsed to assess the working of the scheme thoughout the Merchant Navy. In this he showed his wisdom, for many experiments in human relations are successful owing to the high calibre of the men chosen for the experiments.

Unfortunately, in this connection, the Pearson Report[20] also recommended that any seamen brought before the Master for a disciplinary offence should be entitled to have a "friend" present at the hearing. If the liaison representative is the most articulate and knowledgeable man among the crew of a ship he may be the one asked to act as a "friend" to all, if this Pearson recommendation is implemented. This, in turn, may appear to give him some sort of authority and some people fear that the liaison representative may try to interfere in the normal disciplinary procedures aboard the ship.

On the other hand there are advantages to be had from involving the liaison representative in the disciplinary matters of the ship. This representative could be summoned to witness misbehaviour or any acts of disobedience and could then act as a witness during the punishment procedure of "logging" the offender. At the end of the voyage the Master could counteract any persuasive pleas by shore union officials to cancel a fine or logging by calling on the liaison representative—an accredited union representative himself—to substantiate the facts recorded in the log book.

We may well ask why it was felt necessary to introduce these liaison representatives into merchant ships. The main reason was lack of communication between N.U.S. officials ashore and their members at sea, but the union also felt that improvements should be made in the procedure for dealing with the grievances on board ships. The Complaints Procedure was introduced in 1963, but before dealing with this aspect of human relations on board there are two final points to be made about liaison representatives.

The first concerns lack of uniformity in working and living conditions in merchant ships. The *National Maritime Board Year Book*[14] contains comprehensive details on hours of work, wages, overtime and leave, but nowhere does it mention the actual work to be done by each man nor does it describe the facilities and furnishings which a seaman may demand or expect. The result is a complete lack of uniformity in British ships. Some ships supply the crew with matches while others do not; some ships are fitted with swimming pools and others are not; in some ships the morning coffee break, better known as smokho, is 15 minutes while in other ships it is 30 minutes. Anyone who has served as Chief Officer will know that whatever length of time he grants to the crew for smokho, the crew will always say that they were given 5 minutes longer in their last ship, or with the last Mate. Everyone at sea knows that paragon of all virtues, the "last ship" and, if complaints prefaced with "In my last ship we did this or that . . ."

are to be avoided, a comprehensive and clearly worded book will have to be drawn up stating exactly what the crew may demand and what they may not. Comprehensive "Labour Awards" which describe, in the smallest detail, the living, working and employment conditions to be granted on board, have been in use in Australian and New Zealand ships for many years. A similar labour award or code of practice will need to be drawn up for British ships before the powers of liaison representatives are increased.

The second point concerns interviews between the Master and the liaison representative. The point was made in Chapter 3 that, if a representative were given the right of private interview with the Master, he could undermine the Master's authority by giving to the crew a somewhat coloured version of what passed between him and the "Old Man". One way of overcoming this problem would be for the Master to insist on the representative presenting his complaints to the Master before a committee of members drawn from all sections of the ship's company. Another way would be for the Master to insist on witnesses being present at all interviews between himself and the liaison representative.

The Complaints Procedure

However well a ship may be organized and however good her accommodation may be, some complaints are sure to arise. The nature of the ship's trade or the need for discipline may prove to be irksome to an individual. It is most important that, whether the grievance is genuine or not, the man concerned is given a satisfactory answer as soon as possible after the event which gave rise to the grievance. Crew morale is reduced if grievances are allowed to fester.

Both shipowners and unions recognized the need to introduce a scheme whereby complaints could be dealt with speedily and satisfactorily and, in 1963, the National Maritime Board adopted the official Complaints Procedure. The whole purpose behind the adoption of this scheme was to create a proper channel through which any member of a ship's company could take his complaint to the person who had the power to deal with it.

Any man who has a grievance should make his complaint to his head of section. A deck rating, for example, would make it to the Bosun. The head of section should try to deal with the complaint but, if it is beyond his power to deal with the particular complaint or if the complainant so requests, the matter will be taken to the head of that man's department. The complaint from a deck rating, to follow the example used here, would be taken to the Chief Officer who should interview the rating in the presence of the head of section.

If the complainant is still not satisfied he may request to see the Master and the head of department should arrange for this to be done. If the Master cannot deal with the complaint, or if the complainant is still not satisfied, then the complaint may, at the complainant's request, be forwarded in writing to the management of the shipping company. If, in addition, the complainant wants to communicate with his union or association, the Master should afford him the necessary facilities for doing so.

In ships with large crews it may be found more convenient for the heads of section to record any complaints and for the heads of departments to inspect these records once a week or more often. Each head of department will try to satisfy any complaints coming from the men in his department, but, if he cannot satisfy any complaint, the matter will be taken up with the Master or, if necessary, with the management of the company.

If a complaint involves another department, a representative from that department should be present when the matter is being investigated by the head of department.

No-one on board ship has the power to alter any National Maritime Board agreement and, if any complaint concerns the interpretation of a clause in the N.M.B. agreements, the matter should be deferred until it can be handled by the shipowners' and seafarer's organizations.

No man making a complaint in good faith and in accordance with the Official Procedure should be penalized in any way.

Furthermore, the existence of this Procedure does not preclude any man from making a request to see his head of department or the Master on a private matter.

Under Sections 198 and 211 of the Merchant Shipping Act 1894[13] and under section 35 of the Merchant Shipping (Crew Accommodation) Regulations, seamen may lodge complaints on provisions, water, accommodation, and alleged unseaworthiness and ill treatment before a proper authority. This proper authority may be a superintendent of a Mercantile Marine Office, a British consul, a Board of Trade surveyor, or an officer commanding one of Her Majesty's ships. A proper authority receiving such a complaint must institute a survey or investigation of the matter and the results of this survey must be entered in the ship's official log book. While seamen do have the legal right to lodge complaints under the Merchant Shipping Act they should only take such action when conditions aboard become intolerable and the complaints cannot be resolved in any other manner. Proper use of the N.M.B. Complaints Procedure should make the lodging of complaints under the Merchant Shipping Act quite unnecessary.

Disputes over wages, overtime payments, leave pay, or over any other cause may arise when the crew sign off a ship at the end of the voyage. If the amount involved in the dispute between one man and the Master is less than £5, the Superintendent of the Mercantile Marine Office, before whom the men are discharged, has the power (under Section 137 of the Merchant Shipping Act, 1894) to settle the claim. If the amount involved is over £5, or if the dispute concerns matters other than wages, the Superintendent may arbitrate only if both parties agree, in writing, to submit the matter to him.

CHAPTER 9

Selection, Recruitment and Promotion

THERE are various ways of estimating the costs of education, but when the real cost of teaching, the costs of accommodation, wages paid and wages foregone, and administrative costs are all added together, the total real cost of training an engineer officer (in 1968) from cadet to Chief Engineer lies in the region of £9000 while the cost of training a navigating officer from cadet to Master is about £6600. Of these sums, the shipowner pays out about £4000 for the training of an engineer cadet under the Alternative Entry Scheme and about £2400 for the training of a navigating cadet.

The total annual cost of nautical training in Britain during 1968 lay in the region of £9 million and we must ask ourselves if the shipping industry and the state are getting a proper return on their training investments.

The average length of time spent at sea by the members of one particular group can be found from the formula:

$$\text{Average length of time} = \int_{0}^{40} e^{-kt}\, dt$$

where t is in years, and $e^{-k} = \dfrac{100 - \text{percentage loss}}{100}$. The true percentage loss is obtained by correcting the raw percentage by a factor of

$$\dfrac{100 - \dfrac{\text{re-entrants}}{\text{loss}}}{100}.$$

The raw percentage is given by:

$$100 \times \frac{\text{Group strength at start of year} + \text{New recruits} + \text{Re-entrants} +}{\text{Group strength at start of year} + \text{New recruits} + \text{Re-entrants} +}$$

$$\frac{\text{Men promoted into group} - \text{Group strength at end of year}}{\text{Men promoted into group}}$$

Using this formula, we find that the average length of time spent at sea by all navigating officers and cadets is 6·5 years (13 years for certificated officers only) and by all engineer officers is 6·0 years (9·5 years for certificated engineer officers only).

The figures above show that £9000 is spent on training an engineer officer for 6·0 years at sea and £6600 on training a navigating officer for 6·5 years at sea. This, in turn, shows that if shipowners are to get a proper return on their training investments the greatest care should be taken in selecting cadets and a great deal of effort must be put into removing or reducing those factors which cause men to leave the sea at an early age.

Marriage is usually given as the most important cause of men leaving the sea, and some people explain away the wastage of unmarried cadets by saying that the young men of today cannot stand the rigours and demands of a life at sea and that they prefer a life of "pop" music and coffee bars ashore. These reasons for wastage are in partial conflict with the results of a survey I carried out in 1965. This survey was carried out in order to determine the incentives which attracted men to a career at sea.

It appears that, among recruits and cadets in the 16–21 age-group, the incentives to go to sea are escape from a boring home routine and a sense of adventure. Among young deck officers in the 22–33 age-group, the biggest single incentive to stay at sea is the prospect of getting command and amongst older deck officers (over 38 years old) the incentive to stay at sea is an economic one—many of these men are building up comfortable homes ashore and simply cannot afford to leave the sea. An interesting aspect of the survey was the change of incentive from adventure to prospect of command. This change takes place during the last year of a boy's apprenticeship or during his first year as a watchkeeping officer when he suddenly realizes that the Master is the top of the deck officer group and is not some strange and remote being. The desire for command comes more from a desire to succeed than from a desire for power, and this feeling is strongest in the 21–33 age-group. If the prospect of getting command were taken away from the men in this age-group at sea today, then it is likely that many of those men would leave the sea.

During an earlier research programme carried out to determine the reasons for men leaving the sea, frustration ranked high on the list. As was mentioned earlier in this book, frustration exists when a man sees a block between what he has and what he feels he is entitled to. Many shipping companies hold out the prospect of command as an attraction when recruiting deck cadets. Not only are they wrong to suggest that every boy going to sea as a cadet should eventually rise to command, but such a suggestion actually increases frustration. The cadet, on getting his Second Mate's Certificate and reaching officer status, sees ahead of him, on the company's rank list, scores of names and he knows that, under the present system of promotion on seniority only, nothing he can do will enable him to overtake those ahead of him on the rank list and enable him to reach his goal—command—any earlier. This is what causes frustration among young officers and causes them to leave the sea. If frustration is to be reduced, then a system of promotion on merit must be introduced throughout the Merchant Navy, as is already being done by some companies. Prospect of command should not be held out to every boy who joins the Merchant Navy, but each recruit should be clearly told that he will only reach command if he is good enough.

Methods of promotion on merit will be described later in this chapter, but first we should examine methods of selecting the right boys.

The traditional methods of selecting boys for the Merchant Navy are well known: a very common method is for a boy to write to a shipping company and, provided he holds approximately the right academic qualifications, he is then summoned to an interview at the company's office. In some companies, this interview is carried out by the Marine Superintendent who, quite often, is far too busy with other things to be able to devote as much time as he would like to the selection interview. In some other companies the boy is interviewed by a shore clerk who has only the haziest ideas of what life at sea is really like. The choice of whether the boy should go into the deck, engine-room or catering departments is usually left entirely to the boy or his parents with little guidance from the shipping company and with absolutely no measurements of his aptitudes being taken. Worst of all is that, in many cases, little thought is given to the boy's future should he want to leave the sea—the only hope in the interviewer's mind being that this boy will stay at sea for a reasonable length of time.

Some leading companies devote a great deal of effort to their recruitment interviews while one particular company, Irish Shipping Limited, uses a panel of sea staff and a full battery of properly designed tests in order to select the right recruits. It is imperative for shipping companies to select the right boys if they are to get a reasonable return on the money they invest in training. This selection may be done by a company's own staff or by an independent firm of psychological consultants.

All sound recruitment procedures must, however, be based on a prior job analysis. It is a complete waste of time selecting a boy on the basis of his academic qualifications or on the manner of his dress; such a system could almost be described as a recruitment version of "Russian roulette". If, for any reason, a company cannot afford the cost of carrying out a full job analysis, then the best method it can adopt is to invite a good Master, Chief Engineer, Chief Officer, and junior officer to interview all applicants. Between them, these officers should be able to select the most suitable boys, and inviting a panel of sea staff to assist with the selection interviews has the added advantage of bringing the shore and sea sections of the company closer together and of stopping complaints from the sea staff about the quality of the new recruits.

The aim in carrying out a full job analysis is to define exactly what a man has to do in a particular job and what personality and ability factors make him suitable for that job. It is only after all these factors are known that proper selection can be made.

There are a number of ways of carrying out this job analysis. One way is by engaging trained psychologists and work study experts to carry out observations on board the company's ships. Another way is for the company itself to carry out this analysis by defining each job as closely as possible and then sending out questionnaires to as many men as possible. These carefully designed questionnaires should ask, for a particular job or role, what physical work the man needs to do; what mental work he has to do; what knowledge he needs and what abilities he should have.

The questionnaires should be very carefully worded in order to avoid ambiguity. The best way of explaining this method is by means of an example. Let us imagine that we were wanting to define the job of a Third Officer. Questionnaires should be sent to as many Masters, Deck Officers and others who deal with Third Officers as possible. Each recipient should be asked to describe the actual work done by a Third Officer and the abilities needed to carry out this work. For example, the Third Officer keeps a bridge watch for eight hours a day and must be able to stay alert for that length of time; he must have good eyesight and must not be colour blind; he must be able to lay off bearings on a chart and must, therefore, be neat and precise; he must have sufficient mathematical ability to work out the ship's position from astronomical sights; he has to check life-boat equipment and other life-saving appliances without supervision and must, therefore, be methodical and trustworthy; in port he has to keep a cargo watch, which means that he will have to execute orders given to him by the Chief Officer—he should accept these orders cheerfully and not with sullen resentment; he must have the courage to be firm with would-be pilferers of cargo; he should be punctual when relieving the watch; he should be of sober habits in order to carry out his duties properly; in passenger ships he may have to deal with passengers and should, therefore, have some social polish. There are many other factors which should be included in the questionnaire. Those answering these questionnaires should also be asked to state what factors make the present incumbent of the post better or worse than his predecessors.

The completed questionnaires should then be analysed by a job evaluation committee composed of trained shore staff and experienced sea staff. This committee will need to weigh the various factors, for the views of sea staff and shore management may not coincide on what makes a good Third Officer. The sea staff may value a Third Officer's ability to arrange parties in port while shore management would attach more weight to his performance on cargo watch! Another thing this committee would have to do is to analyse accidents or incidents involving Third Officers in order to determine what went wrong and why it did. The purpose of this last analysis is to determine what qualities should be in Third Officers if similar accidents are to be avoided in the future.

Similar analyses should be carried out for all the jobs aboard ship in order to show the selectors what to look for when interviewing applicants. The management of a company may attach some importance to keeping the boy at sea for a reasonable length of time. In this case a full assessment will have to be made of the home background and personality factors which appear to be common to those officers who have stayed at sea the longest. These factors can best be determined by sending out questionnaires designed to get information on each man's background before he went to sea—the type of school he attended, whether his home was inland or near the sea, what sort of sports he played, what company he kept, the disciplinary system in his home, and many other similar factors. The personality of these officers can best be measured by using one of the well-validated standard personality questionnaires so that the "personality profile" of the ideal officer may be drawn up. These personality and home profiles are further yardsticks for the selectors.

Even when the desirable qualities have been defined, the selectors may still have difficulty in assessing these qualities in the applicants. The best way of overcoming this problem is by using a suitably designed battery of written and practical tests. Many well-validated tests are on the market; a shipping company will simply have to choose those which best suit its requirements. Some tests measure mental ability while others measure mental alertness. Some measure mechanical ability while others measure manual dexterity. The advice of a trained psychologist should be sought in order to decide which tests should be used, in fact some tests may only be applied by a properly qualified person. These written and practical tests should be used to supplement the findings of the interview panel which, as was said earlier, should be composed of experienced sea staff and trained shore staff.

It may be of interest to the reader to hear of a selection procedure I developed for Irish Shipping Limited in 1966. A preliminary meeting was held with the management of the company in order to get information on the importance they attached to the various factors affecting efficiency and length of service at sea. Questionnaires were sent out to a cross-section of the officers in their ships in order to draw up the "personality, attitudes and background profiles" of the ideal officer. The Maudsley Personality Inventory was used to measure Introversion/Extroversion and Stability/Neuroticism. (Both Deck and Engineer Officers were found to be extremely stable but, while Deck Officers were slightly introverted, the Engineer Officers proved to be slightly extroverted.)

Once the profiles had been established, a battery of tests were designed. These were aimed at measuring the same factors as were found in the sea staff profiles; at measuring Divergency/Convergency of thinking processes; at measuring spatial reasoning ability; and at measuring attitudes which would make life at sea acceptable or unacceptable to the applicant.

We had 123 applicants for ten deck and ten engineering vacancies. Each day twelve boys were invited to attend and they were divided into two groups of six. While one group completed the paper tests and were interviewed by the panel of sea and shore staff, the other group was put through a series of practical tests similar to those used by the Armed Services in Britain. The equipment used for these tests consisted of a few empty drums, rope, spars, blocks, cargo nets, and bits of machinery. For some tests a leader was appointed while, for other tests, no leader was officially appointed and observations were made on who was thrown up by the group as their natural leader. All the tests consisted of practical problems, the solution of which called for originality of thought, clear orders by the leader, and hard work by all. Observations were made on the boy's ability to lead, his readiness to work and on his problem-solving ability. The points scored at these practical tests were weighed and added to the weighed results of the paper tests before the final score was obtained. The final selection of boys obtained from these tests was compared with the selection made by the interview panel and a high degree of correlation was found to exist. (The correlation may have been due to both myself and the interviewers being experienced seamen.)

The correct selection of cadets is probably the most important step a shipping company needs to take in improving its human resources. After selection and training comes another important step—promotion.

In the Merchant Navy today, most promotion is based on length of service rather than on merit although, it should be mentioned, if a man is in the right place at the right time he may enjoy accelerated promotion. As things are at sea today, length of service for promotional purposes is usually based on the length of service in a particular company and many people outside the shipping industry are amazed to learn that shipping companies rarely take into account a man's service in another company.

Promotion on length of service is harmful in a number of ways:

it is a source of frustration to the more able young officers; it may mean that, just through sheer length of service, a man may be promoted to a senior position for which he is not really fitted; and it suppresses initiative—for men become more interested in keeping their records clean than in doing anything out of the ordinary.

Some men object to promotion on merit on the grounds that such a system is open to abuse and that, even if it were done fairly, those officers who have been "passed over" will leave the sea. Neither objection is really valid for merit systems can be introduced which are free of abuse and, even if some of the "passed over" officers leave the sea, many more able officers will stay at sea if they think their ability and diligence will be rewarded.

The greater bulk of Merchant Navy officers of average ability would not be affected by a system of promotion on merit except that, when they see their more able colleagues enjoying accelerated promotion, they will be spurred to greater efforts. The really weak officers would probably leave the sea. The whole of the shipping industry will be the better for the introduction of a promotion-on-merit scheme.

It should be mentioned that, while they still value long and faithful service, some leading shipping companies are already taking merit into account when deciding upon promotions.

There are three ways of carrying out promotion on merit. The first is by engaging a firm of independent psychologists to determine which men are of command material and then to promote on that basis. The second method is for the company to set an internal written examination aimed at measuring an officer's knowledge of his company's procedure and of the peculiarities of the trade in which he is engaged. Great care must be taken in the designing of such an examination for it should not overlap, in any way, the examinations for certificates of competency set by the Board of Trade. If it does overlap, the officers may object to having to pass the same examinations twice, and their Associations would probably support their objections. The third, and most effective, way is to base promotion on reports from Masters, senior officers and Superintendents.

If promotion is to be based on Master's reports then the reports currently used by many shipping companies will need to be vastly improved. Furthermore, those Masters and senior officers who have to make these reports will need to be instructed and trained in reporting procedures. These senior men will need to be given a clear understanding of what is required of them; they will have to work to a common standard; and they will have to take their reporting role seriously.

Many shipping companies today require confidential reports to be made on all their company service contract employees but, in very many cases, the report forms used simply list a number of items—such as punctuality, efficiency, sobriety, and dress, and the reporting officer is allowed to complete them, with minimum effort on his part, by putting "Average" against each item.

It is most important that a report is shown to the officer concerned before it is despatched to the company's head office; it is also important that the company's report tallies with the official report given to the man in his discharge book. There have been a number of cases where the management of a company has summoned an officer to the head office for a reprimand on his insobriety only to find that the officer concerned knew nothing about the adverse report and, in fact, could refute it by showing the "V.G." report in his discharge book.

Shipping companies should be able to design their own report forms for only they will know what weight they attach to the various factors of performance and personality. Sound report forms can only be based on a true job analysis as described earlier in this chapter. One type of report is reproduced on the following pages. It could be modified, if necessary, and used by any shipping company.

—— Shipping Company

Report made by: Confidential report on:
Name   Name
Rank   Rank or Rating
                                         Name of ship
                                         Professional qualifications:—

Instructions: Place a tick between the brackets opposite the most appropriate
statement.

CHARACTER AND PERSONALITY

1. *Working under stress*
    Never panics, always calm and sure.   ( )
    Works well under stress.   ( )
    Rarely displays panic.   ( )
    Nervous in some situations.   ( )
    Very nervous in all stress situations, panics easily.   ( )
2. *Responsibility for results*
    Seeks responsibility.   ( )
    Always willing to accept responsibility.   ( )
    Only accepts responsibility when absolutely necessary.   ( )
    Prefers someone else to take charge.   ( )
    Avoids taking responsibility.   ( )
3. *Responsibility for errors*
    Accepts criticism in good grace.   ( )
    Accepts criticism reasonably well.   ( )
    Does not always accept valid criticism.   ( )
    Seeks excuses for his own errors.   ( )
    Resents criticism, always blames someone else.   ( )
4. *Working under uncomfortable conditions*
    Accepts such work cheerfully.   ( )
    Accepts such work when necessary.   ( )
    Only carries out exactly what he has to do.   ( )
    Displays dislike for work in uncomfortable conditions.   ( )
    Usually tries to escape such work.   ( )
5. *Taking orders*
    Carries out the spirit of the order.   ( )
    Accepts orders reasonably well.   ( )
    Only does exactly what he is ordered to do.   ( )
    Accepts orders in bad grace.   ( )
    Becomes sullen and resentful when ordered to do something. ( )
6. *Sobriety*
    Complete teetotaler.   ( )
    Rarely touches alcohol.   ( )
    Only drinks outside hours of duty.   ( )
    Occasionally drink affects his performance.   ( )
    His performance is frequently affected by alcohol.   ( )

PERFORMANCE OF HIS DUTIES

1. *Working*
Usually does more than he has to do.   ( )
Does more when the job interests him.   ( )
Carries out his duties satisfactorily.   ( )
Dislikes work.   ( )
Tries to escape work and leaves it to others.   ( )

2. *Interest in the work of the ship*
Displays interest in all the work of the ship.   ( )
Displays interest in the work of his department.   ( )
Displays interest only in his own job.   ( )
Does not display interest even in his own job.   ( )
Is completely disinterested in everything concerning the ship
  and his own job.   ( )

3. *Punctuality*
Always on duty well before the time required.   ( )
Often on duty before the time required.   ( )
Punctual for his times of duty.   ( )
Sometimes late for his time of duty.   ( )
Frequently late for his time of duty.   ( )

4. *Delegation of work to others*
Delegates work sensibly to his subordinates.   ( )
Delegates some work to his subordinates.   ( )
Only delegates work when he is too busy.   ( )
Rarely delegates work to others.   ( )
Never delegates work to others; deals with everything himself.   ( )

5. *Interest in training his juniors*
Does all he can to prepare men below for promotion.   ( )
Is always ready to help and train juniors.   ( )
Carries out his training function reasonably well.   ( )
Does not display much interest in training his juniors.   ( )
Refuses to train his juniors in any way.   ( )

6. *Management of subordinates*
Inspires men to give of their best.   ( )
Manages men well.   ( )
Men work quite well for him.   ( )
He does not manage and control his men well.   ( )
He handles his subordinates very badly.   ( )

7. *Organization of work*
Exceptionally good organizer.   ( )
Quite skilful at planning work.   ( )
Plans work reasonably well.   ( )
His work planning is frequently poor.   ( )
He cannot organize work plans.   ( )

8. *Feedback of information*
Keeps superiors fully informed on all happenings.   ( )
Volunteers information.   ( )
Only gives information when asked for it.   ( )
Does not give full information on all topics.   ( )
Rarely gives information, usually tries to cover up.   ( )

9. *Accuracy of work*
Exceptionally accurate and precise.   ( )
Neat and accurate.   ( )
Reasonably accurate.   ( )
Often wrong in his calculations.   ( )
Rarely correct; his work should be checked by someone else. ( )

10. *Order giving*
His orders are clear and precise.   ( )
He gives orders well.   ( )
The men usually know what he wants to be done.   ( )
He gives orders badly.   ( )
He is clumsy in order giving.   ( )

11. *Firmness*
He is very firm with men who misbehave.   ( )
He is usually firm and fair.   ( )
He is firm only when required to be so.   ( )
He often shuts his eye to acts of indiscipline.   ( )
He is soft and has lost control of his men.   ( )

A. *From reporting officer*
I strongly wish to have this man under my command again. ( )
I would be pleased to have this man under my command again. ( )
I would have this man under my command again if necessary. ( )
I would prefer to have another man in his place.   ( )
I would not have this man under my command again under
    any circumstances.   ( )

B. *Promotion*
I recommend this man for promotion immediately.   ( )
I recommend this man for promotion soon.   ( )
This man may be promoted after further experience.   ( )
This man should not be promoted beyond his present position. ( )
This man should be demoted or expelled from the company ( )

Signature of reporting officer: ....

I declare that I have read through this report:

Signature of man on whom report has been made: ....

CHAPTER 10

Education—an Overall View

by J. ANDREW DAVIES

What is education?

Education can be defined as the process by which a person is
enabled to deal more effectively with his environment. It includes
the acquisition of knowledge and experience, and the personal
development of each individual. This is a very broad and all-
embracing definition, and it indicates that education must never
be thought of as something which ceases the moment a person
leaves school or college; it is a lifelong continuing process.

A well-educated person is one who possesses knowledge and
experience, plus the ability to apply effectively his knowledge and
experience in any situation. He will be prepared to adapt his
environment as necessary, and will also adapt himself to his
environment. For example, he will extract maximum interest from
a seemingly boring and mundane situation, but will also deal
effectively with any unforeseen circumstance or emergency that
might arise.

Having briefly considered this idealistic, all-embracing definition, let us shift to the other end of the spectrum and consider the
shipowner. How is the shipowner likely to view education? The
shipowner is primarily interested in keeping sufficient of the
"right" people at sea in order to run his existing and future ships
efficiently and economically, so at first sight it might appear that
he shipowner will be mainly concerned with a narrow and limited
vocational training. However, it follows from the above description of a well-educated person that education has a major role to

play in attracting people to the sea, and helping to keep them content when at sea, since the efficient operation of ships is dependent on the efforts of well-adapted (as well as trained) personnel. For further illustration we must consider the development of our educational system and the specific functions of education.

The educational system in
England and Wales

Compulsory full-time education for all was introduced as a result of the 1870 Education Act, although the implementation of the Act was not completed until about twenty-five years later. Full-time education was seen as a means of preparing citizens to occupy their "station in life"—largely pre-determined by the home and family circumstances. State secondary education developed gradually following the 1902 Education Act and the formation of Local Education Authorities. We see that the educational system has mushroomed over the last hundred years, and is now a major industry. Periods of rapid growth in the system have tended to occur when the government and industry have compared our society with the societies of our trading competitors and found that we were falling behind in scientific, industrial or technological progress, and in the provision of educational facilities. This is well illustrated in the Robbins Report on Higher Education[19] in 1963, from which the following extracts are taken.

Paragraph 16. . . . the growing realisation of this country's economic dependence upon the education of its population has led to much questioning of the adequacy of present arrangements. Unless higher education is speedily reformed, it is argued, there is little hope of this densely populated island maintaining an adequate position in the fiercely competitive world of the future.

Paragraph 25. And it must be recognised that, in our own times, progress—and particularly the maintenance of a competitive position—depends to a much greater extent than ever before on skills demanding special training. A good general education, valuable though it may be, is frequently less than we need to solve many of our most pressing problems.

Paragraph 26. . . . we must postulate that what is taught should be taught in such a way as to promote the general powers of the mind. The aim should be to produce not mere specialists but rather cultivated men and women.

Paragraph 28. . . . we believe that it is a proper function of higher education, as of education in schools, to provide in partnership with the family that background of culture and social habit upon which a healthy society depends.

Paragraph 130. (Comparing the expansion of higher education in Great Britain with the expansion in other countries.) But at the present time the conclusion is plain: the comparison of numbers likely to qualify is no longer favourable, and the disparity in the numbers entering higher education is even wider than it is today. Both in general cultural standards and in competitive intellectual power, vigorous action is needed to avert the danger of a serious relative decline in this country's standing.

Implementation of the main recommendations of this report is now well under way, and is having its effects within nautical education, e.g. degrees in nautical studies awarded by the Council for National Academic Awards.

It is now generally accepted that unless a country is very rich in natural resources its wealth is largely dependent on the provision of educational facilities. The following figures, taken from the latest report of the Department of Education and Science[18], illustrate the rate of expansion of our own education system.

The share of national resources used by the education service in the United Kingdom in the mid-sixties was $5\frac{1}{2}$ per cent, compared with $3\frac{1}{2}$ per cent of considerably smaller resources ten years earlier. Total annual expenditure over the period rose from £560 million in 1954–55 to £1784 million in 1965–66. Students in further education increased by a half to reach $2\frac{3}{4}$ million. In 1965–66 the total number of students following courses of higher education in Great Britain was over 300,000.

Massive expansion of educational provision is already one of the incontrovertible facts of social and economic history in the sixties.

In secondary education, boys of moderate ability and above are encouraged to stay on at school until 17 or 18, and it has become difficult to recruit such boys into the shipping industry at 16. Again quoting from the above report[18],

PROPORTIONS OF 15-, 16- AND 17-YEAR-OLD PUPILS IN MAIN-
TAINED SCHOOLS IN ENGLAND AND WALES, as PERCENTAGES
OF THE AGE GROUP

January	Age 15	Age 16	Age 17
1959	29·2	14·6	7·0
1962	33·9	16·6	8·6
1966	54·6	22·0	11·0

This trend is bound to continue and grow, as every boy is made aware of the improvement in his life chances which result from extended education.

Increasing interest is also being shown in those aspects of education which have some direct vocational significance. In the United Kingdom, the Industrial Training Act of 1964[7] has resulted in the formation of Training Boards for the major industries, these Boards being charged with the duty of developing all aspects of training. There are now about twenty of these Boards, representing industries employing some ten million workers.

The Merchant Navy relies for its survival against international competition on recruits who are the product of our present educational system, and who have usually experienced some form of vocational training. In order to evaluate the quality of recruits to the industry we must consider the exact functions of the educational system in our society.

Functions of the educational system

These may be listed as:
1. To transmit the culture of the society. (The word "culture" embraces the total social, intellectual and artistic develop-ment of the group.)
2. To improve each individual's life chances.
3. To increase the individual's ability to
    (a) profit from experience, and
    (b) deal effectively with the opportunities offered by his environment.

Much discussion has taken place concerning the relative importance of these functions, but I suggest that we steer clear of such value judgements and simply regard all three functions as necessary and therefore important.

1. To transmit the culture of the society. This function can be fulfilled by what we can refer to as "general" education. A number of factors need to be considered under this heading.

(a) Every ten years the amount of knowledge in the world doubles. Twenty years from now there will be four times as much knowledge available as there is today. This indicates the necessity for longer and longer schooling, and a shift in emphasis away from simple storage of factual information by the individual towards the development of the ability to search out relevant information and process it. This calls for a flexible, problem-solving approach and a questioning attitude to any given situation.

(b) Technological development results in a decreasing need for manual workers and a changing pattern of available jobs and careers. A good general education enables an individual to appreciate the need for, and to cope with, a changing environment. It has already become necessary to re-train some of the working members of our society (e.g. miners, railwaymen), and this trend is bound to increase. In fact, some people may have to change their jobs several times during their working lives.

(c) Members of society are enjoying increasing amounts of leisure time and longer retirement. Opportunities for travel, holidays, pursuit of hobbies and interests exist for everyone, and individuals who have had a good general education can make the most of such opportunities.

(d) Children must be educated to understand the role of each individual in the society, and the part that they must play in the development of that society.

As previously mentioned, official reports stress the need for more and more general education, but this does not mean "University for all". Indeed, many present sixth-form pupils are taking general courses not aimed at G.C.E. "A"-level examinations,

and there is a growing trend away from too much narrow specialization in sixth form studies. California has been toying with the
idea of a normal school-leaving age of twenty, and, in the U.S.A.
as a whole, students who leave high school before the age of
eighteen are regarded as "drop-outs" from the system.

2. To improve each individual's life chances. This second
function of education is to provide each individual with the
necessary basic skills and qualifications which will enable him
to progress in his chosen career. With the shift from heredity to
ability as the prime factor governing success in a career, the
tendency is to use qualifications as the yardstick for assessing a
person's ability and suitability for a position. The exact "value"
of a particular qualification can therefore be determined without
too much difficulty. This technique has become a fine art in
the U.S.A., where comparisons are made between the lifetime's
earnings of people possessing/not possessing, say, a Ph.D. We live
in a competitive society, and it is the job of the educational
system to provide people with the qualifications which will
enable them to compete to the best of their abilities.

It could be argued that the first function deals with general
education and the second with vocational education, but this is
not a clear-cut distinction, e.g. a General Certificate in Education
and a Bachelor of Arts degree are not vocational qualifications, but possession of these would improve an individual's life
chances.

To digress slightly, as vocational education has just been mentioned, the reader might have noticed that the word "training"
has not yet been used, apart from brief references to vocational
training and the Industrial Training Boards. This is because
training can be considered to be simply a part of education—as
education has been defined for the purpose of this chapter.
Training versus education arguments can arise unless we define
the scope of the two words. Training *can* be defined as the process
by which a person acquires some mechanical skill with few
variables, enabling him to cope with an essentially practical
situation, for example training a person to tie a reef-knot, or

make an eye-splice in a wire rope. However, the word training is often used when referring to "vocational education", for example teacher-training. Training is even used to apply to the development of the individual's personality, as in character-training. The Industrial Training Act empowers an industrial training board to consider employment in the industry concerned and publish recommendations governing the further education to be associated with training, thereby extending the scope of the board beyond basic-skill training. All training can therefore be included within the total sphere of the word education.

3. To increase the individual's ability to
(a) profit from experience, and
(b) deal effectively with the opportunities offered by his environment.

This third function is really the heart of the whole process of education, since education must have as its ultimate aim the well-being of the individual and the society. This function could even be said to incorporate the first two stated functions, although it is often overlooked in normal day-to-day living.

The first two functions deal with the more practical aspects of education whereas this one appears to be somewhat nebulous, but on inspection it will be found to be the most important for the self-fulfilment and development of the individual. The ability to profit from experience is closely related to intelligence, and it is interesting to see that Sir Edward Boyle, in the Foreword to the Newsom Report[17], *Half our Future*, says:

The essential point is that all children should have an equal opportunity of *acquiring intelligence*, and of developing their talents and abilities to the full.

Successful adaptation to life at sea can best be ensured by means of education which is aimed at increasing the seafarer's ability to deal effectively with the opportunities offered by his environment. The type of education necessary to achieve this end cannot be defined precisely, but several useful pointers can be given. Self-expression and the art of critical analysis must be encouraged and developed. Students must be stimulated to develop powers of divergent, as well as convergent, thinking, in order to extract the maximum interest from any situation. Unfortunately, many situations in education encourage convergent thinking, where the student's thoughts are channelled towards a single "correct" solution, e.g.

Hat is to head as shoe is to . . .

Solve for x, $2x^2+11x+12=0$

Tests using this type of material are used because they can be marked quickly and objectively, but how much more rewarding and stimulating are questions which involve divergent thinking, e.g.

How many uses can you think of for a hat (or a brick, or a blanket)?

Creativity, the ability to interpret and re-structure information, extrapolating and developing a given situation, needs to be encouraged whenever possible. Many problems in seamanship, and particularly those involving leadership of a group, require the exercise of creativity (based on knowledge and experience) to adapt existing materials to new uses. The development of a society is often largely dependent on the efforts of a highly creative people, and this is true for scientific as well as for artistic endeavours.

It must be remembered that there is an immense difference between life ashore, with its wide variety of leisure activities, and life on board a ship, with its restrictions and limitations. The contrast has increased considerably due to mass communication media and improved standards of living. A seafarer spends long periods in the narrow confines of a ship. His working routine is monotonous and opportunities for entertainment are very restricted. Generally speaking, the seafarer has no television, no newspapers, no current magazines, no sports, no motor car, no pubs, no family life, no theatres or cultural group activities, no educational facilities. One wonders how the average person ashore would react if so deprived. The seafarer is, therefore, much more dependent on his own resources, but at the same time he is not subject to the variety of distractions which exist ashore. A seafarer who has developed an absorbing hobby is much more likely to be content with his life at sea.

The seafarer enjoys unique opportunities to study certain subjects at first hand, e.g. geography, languages. Every seafarer should study at least a few aspects of some subject in depth. I have spoken to a number of officers who, after some years at sea, have studied a subject in depth and who then realize that they wasted many opportunities while at sea and went around "with their eyes shut". Once a person has decided to go to sea, he should be given opportunities to develop interests other than those of a narrow vocational nature. It is equally the duty of anyone concerned with the education of seafarers to try to motivate them to become autonomous, self-propelled thinkers, so that studies can be continued at sea away from the direct influence of tutors. The attitude of regarding oneself as a life-long learner must be instilled into each individual.

Modern developments in education

The next question to be asked is "Are there any recent developments in education which can contribute towards the ideals already mentioned?" Here the answer is a most emphatic "Yes". Modern techniques, made possible by technological development, were relatively slow to influence educational method, but during the last ten or so years progress has been rapid and the pace is an ever increasing one. The population explosion, the needs of developing countries, and a world-wide shortage of teachers have resulted in improved techniques of self-instruction, e.g. more and better textbooks, teaching machines and programmed texts, tapes, records, films and film strips. These techniques can be incorporated in or used to replace the traditional type of correspondence course—which has been found to be of limited use for seagoing students, mainly due to the lack of intrinsic motivation provided by the course and the long delay between completing work and getting it back from the tutor.

Psychological research has led to increased understanding of the learning process—in fact the principles for writing the first programmes used in teaching machines were based largely on the work of B. F. Skinner, Professor of Psychology at Harvard University. The use of programmed texts by seafarers is almost certain to increase, and this will enable them to study effectively without outside help. A programmed text consists of a carefully planned and sequenced course of self-instruction, which has been comprehensively tested and revised until it achieves the desired results, and with which the student is engaged in frequent active responding as he works through the material. Responses are checked by the student as he proceeds, and the knowledge of results obtained provides motivation and assists learning. The student proceeds at his own pace, and success is guaranteed, as a result of trying out and revising the programme before publication until it is found to be successful.

Tape recorders are now available which can be used as portable language laboratories. The top track of the tape contains the lesson and cannot be erased while on the machine. Responses made by the student are recorded on the lower track, and can be played back or erased as desired. Again, instruction is individualized and the student is highly motivated by his involvement with the material. A Belgian merchant ship, the *Montalto*, has recently been fitted with a language laboratory for teaching modern languages to cadets.

A process now coming into use enables video-recordings on film to be played back through any domestic television set via the aerial plug. These films are relatively cheap to produce (compared with video-tape), and it is possible that ships could be supplied with libraries of them. The films are supplied in cassettes or cartridges which are simply inserted into a play-back unit attached to the aerial plug. These films could be included in a programmed course of instruction—as indeed can 35 mm film strips or slides, tape recordings, 8 mm and 16 mm film, depending on the availability of equipment to the programme user and the total cost limitations of the programmed course.

Studying at sea

Unless one is highly motivated by, for example, an absorbing hobby, or by contact with an enthusiast who inspires others with the desire to learn, studying at sea is very difficult. There are always shipmates who will pour scorn on any attempt to study, and those who regard private study as an anti-social activity. Despite the seeming lack of distractions, unless one is on a long sea passage the disturbances in routine caused by having just left port or looking ahead to the next port make it difficult to settle down to studying effectively. In these circumstances it would be foolish to attempt any new work, and the best advice would be to consolidate work already done, by revising notes or scanning through familiar material. Even ten minutes at a time may be found worthwhile, since it will give some sense of achievement and "keep the pot boiling".

Here, now, are some remarks concerning studying. These apply whether one is studying at sea or ashore, for personal ends or for an examination.

1. Getting down to it! As with many activities, the worst aspect of studying is getting started. We tend to put off doing things which we regard as tedious, boring or unpleasant, but once we have started an activity it continues with its own momentum, and often with seemingly little effort, for example shaving, or washing the car. So the trick is to start studying, appreciating that the first couple of minutes are the worst. It helps to have a fixed place of work; a desk with a clear space, a supply of paper, pencils, etc., suitable lighting and heating arrangements. A person should find out whether he works better with the radio on or off, but should avoid becoming too ritualistic —although one very successful writer once admitted that he could never start work until he had sharpened a dozen pencils! Most people study better at certain times of the day; the student should try to find his own best times and establish a habit of studying at those times. It is always a good idea to stop at an interesting point, for example leaving partially solved a problem which the

student knows he can work out completely. This whets the appetite and makes starting again that much easier.

2. Get your aims right. At the start, it pays to establish immediate and long-term goals. Motivation is vital, and a time-table (by providing goals) aids motivation. However, success also aids motivation, so the timetable should not be too ambitious or too rigid. Goals should be attainable, or the final result will simply be frustration. Keep a diary and record of progress. Although it varies somewhat with the subject and type of studying, three hours at one stretch should normally be regarded as an absolute maximum. It is a good idea to break off every hour for a few minutes of relaxation. The student may find it helps to pamper himself with small rewards, for example a cup of coffee at the end of the next problem. Recreation and sleep are important. For most people, burning the midnight oil is unadvisable, since efficiency tends to be low. One should expect good and bad patches, especially if the subject matter is relatively new and unfamiliar. If one has had a break of several weeks or months away from serious mental effort, the first fortnight or so of studying is bound to be difficult and frustrating, and simple mistakes frequent. Unless motivation is very high, studying in isolation may prove to be impossible, in which case the student should try to get someone else to study with him (not necessarily the same subject, but at the same times and possibly in the same room).

3. Reading and note-taking. One should try to develop the reading technique which is most suited to one's personality. One method is to dip into a book, look at chapter headings, intro-duction, notes on authors, etc.; then to scan quickly through sections which catch one's fancy; and finally to read and re-read the book in more detail. Text books are not like novels, since the student can usually enter a textbook at various points other than page one, and the material requires much more careful examina-tion. A useful technique, but one which requires considerable self-discipline, is to read through a page or two of a book and then make notes—having closed the book after reading, and only opening it again if really "stuck". Ideally, the student should

always purchase his own copy of a book, and then he can mark or
underline important statements and passages, and make notes
in the margin. This makes revision from the book easier. (Many
textbooks are now available in cheap paper-backed versions,
which cuts down the cost of building up one's own library.) It
always helps to revise for the first time while the information is
still fresh in the mind, paying particular attention to headings
which can be recalled later on to start off a particular train of
thought.

4.   Learning. When studying a new subject, the mind gradually
acquires a number of items of information and ideas which may
be apparently unconnected. These ideas eventually become sorted
out and categorized and linked together in a complex web.

The degree of meaning which an idea evokes has been shown
to depend on the number and variety of associations which can
be linked to the idea. It is also much easier to learn ideas which
have meaning and which can be linked to other meaningful
ideas. So we have a sort of vicious circle: ideas can only acquire
meaning through the learning of associations, but the associations
are learnt more readily if the ideas have meaning! Fortunately
the two processes tend to run side by side as we acquire mastery
of some new subject matter.

There are various ways in which the student can help himself
to learn. He can get an indexed notebook, and enter in it the
various terms and definitions he comes across, meanings of words,
formulae, etc. Items of information, references, notes on articles
or specific topics can be written down on 4 inch by 6 inch index
cards and then filed in a box under suitable headings or in
alphabetical order. Remember that to be able to find out something by looking it up is often just as important as being able to
recall it. The cards can be used to make up more detailed notes
when they have been sorted out and put in sequence, and they
are useful for revision as well as reference.

A tape recorder is very useful for learning something very
thoroughly. The best way to use it is to record a series of questions.
After each question a suitable pause is left, during which the

student can reply to the question. This is followed by a recording of the correct answer, as a check on the reply. Some pre-recorded tapes dealing with nautical topics are available through the Seafarers' Education Service.

Needs of the shipping industry

Finally, let us consider the effects that developments in the educational system are likely to have on the shipping industry and its needs. We have already seen that the tendency to stay on longer at school must result in either

(a) fewer recruits entering the industry at 16, or
(b) maintaining the same number of recruits by
     (i) lowering the entry standards, or
     (ii) raising the normal entry age.

The final alternative would seem to be the most reasonable one, and it would result in recruits entering the industry at 17 or 18 with higher academic qualifications, i.e. good G.C.E. "O" and probably "A"-levels. This leads to two factors which will have to be considered.

Firstly, the length of cadetships will have to be reduced, since youths of 18 need not, and cannot, be expected to serve for three or four years before achieving officer status. Vocational training will have to be more intensive and closely based on a detailed analysis of an officer's position and function. Simulators may have to be developed which will realistically depict many sea-going situations, so that efficient training can take place under the best conditions (e.g. courses on fire-fighting, safety, man management, cargo work), in order to compress into the least possible training time the whole range of situations which an officer might have to cope with at sea. At the same time, of course, further (general) education must continue as already indicated.

Secondly, older recruits with good G.C.E. results will not be attracted to an industry in which the qualifications offered cannot be related to outside qualifications. With the mobility of labour which exists today, the shipping industry is no longer morally justified in offering such qualifications. As already mentioned under the second function of education, qualifications are carefully graded and judged by society, and individuals are made well aware of their respective merits. This is one reason behind the introduction of the courses leading to a B.Sc. in Nautical Studies, which are already attracting recruits who would not otherwise have entered the shipping industry.

Of course, it could be argued that these higher standard recruits will be less likely to stay at sea, but even so their worth to the industry ashore should prove to be considerable. It is probable that well-educated people are more likely to be contented with a sea-going career, for reasons already stated, but a simple research project could establish where the truth lies—by following through all the people who went to sea in a chosen period and comparing standards of education with lengths of sea-going careers. But that's another story! At present, out of every ten youths who go to sea as deck cadets, only three obtain Master's certificates, and the average total length of sea service (including cadetship) is about seven years, so there are no grounds for complacency.

CHAPTER 11

Nautical Education Today

by A. E. CARVER

Historical background

Organized instruction in navigation in this country may be said to have started in 1673, with the establishment, by Charles II, of the Royal Mathematical Foundation of Christ's Hospital. This was followed by many similar establishments, among which were schools run by the Trinity Houses of Newcastle (1712) and Hull (1785); the latter, of course, is still operating today. These could be regarded as the forerunners of today's cadet training schools, while the private schools, which flourished throughout the 18th and 19th centuries, were the equivalent of today's senior departments. It is interesting to note that this dichotomy persists in the United States, where a few large state and one federal maritime academies train cadets, while officers cram for their licences in private schools.

The law began to take a hand in our maritime training in 1835, when the carrying of apprentices was made compulsory, and the report of a Royal Commission in 1836 recommended the establishment of, *inter alia*, a Mercantile Board examination for officers, registry of seamen, and cheap nautical schools. In the following year an Act of Parliament embodying these recommendations was defeated (the rejection was moved by the then President of the Board of Trade) but in 1845 an Order in Council required the Board of Trade to make arrangements for the voluntary examination of Masters and Mates. This was not strikingly successful, and the examinations were made compulsory in 1851.

Examinations for engineers were instituted in 1862, and

provided for First and Second Class certificates, the latter to take charge of machinery only up to 100 horse power. The Merchant Shipping Act of 1894 brought previous legislation up to date, and remains the most important Act in the seaman's calendar.

Thus the pattern of nautical education in the United Kingdom today has evolved, on the navigating side over three centuries, and on the engineering side over one century. Throughout this time the various interests involved have pursued their own ends, and, at least in the last century, advances have only been achieved by the dogged persistence of the reformers. Standards of the examinations have always been contentious. A Board of Trade circular of 1850 states: "The qualifications (for Mate's and Master's certificates) have been kept as low as possible; but it must be distinctly understood that it is the intention of the Board of Trade to raise the standard from time to time."

The application, in 1862, of "payment by results" to the navigation schools converted them all to cram schools. This system obtained until 1897, and by the end of the century there was an increasing awareness of the deficiencies of the then existing pattern of nautical education. A departmental committee recommended, in 1896, the establishment of training ships or nautical schools for boys, and a series of conferences were held prior to the First World War, which resulted in the Special Regulations for Schools of Nautical Training (1913), and the recognition of five schools under these regulations.

The London School of Nautical Cookery was established in 1893, and, by the Merchant Shipping Act of 1906 it became compulsory for a certificated cook to be carried on each ship. The introduction of wireless telegraphy in 1908 gave the Marconi Company, and later the Postmaster General, an interest in nautical training.

Today's pattern, of colleges with local or central government financial backing, began to be recognizable in the early 1900's and I propose to leave the historical development of this theme in order to describe the schemes of training for the major departments as they are at present.

Cadets

In the deck department, the major source of officers has always been cadets. Out of the 865 Second Mate's certificates awarded in 1966 only 18 went to ex-ratings[a], and it seems possible that this small number will reduce even more. It would be a mistake to close this door of advancement to ratings, but improving methods of selection should be capable of spotting boys suitable for cadet training, and channelling them into appropriate courses.

Engineer cadets are a relatively new feature on the scene, but it is probable that this "alternative" entry will supplant the traditional source of seagoing engineers. Figures quoted below indicate how successful the alternative (cadet) schemes are proving to be in terms of providing certificated engineers. As well as this, the training together of deck and engineer cadets is doing considerable good for inter-departmental relations on board. While 430 Second Class Engineer's certificates were awarded in 1966[b], only four ratings obtained Part A of this certificate. There is a steady throughput of ratings on the two-year course at Leith leading to this certificate, but the numbers from this source do not seem likely to be significant.

Cadets are unknown in the radio department at sea, since radio officers obtain at least their minimum qualifications ashore, before coming to sea. They then come to sea as radio officers, and return ashore as necessary to obtain further qualifications.

Purser and catering cadets are few in number, and their training is geared to the particular needs of their employer's trade.

Deck cadets

There are about 4000 deck cadets in the Merchant Navy[c]. These young men are engaged for three- or four-year periods;

[a]Principal Examiner of Masters and Mates, Board of Trade.
[b]Principal Examiner of Engineers, Board of Trade.
[c]Registrar General of Shipping and Seamen. March 1967 figures: 4072.

the length of the cadetships depending on the remissions granted for certain academic qualifications and recognized pre-sea training. (About half the total number of cadets undergo some sort of pre-sea training.) Although between 1000 and 1200 cadets go to sea each year, only 800 to 900 Second Mate's certificates are awarded annually—this shows that the wastage of deck officers, referred to later in this chapter, starts early.

The trend in the training of deck cadets has been to reduce the length of the pre-sea training period and to introduce a period of release to college at about the middle of the cadetship. Along with this there has been an increase in the average age of boys entering the sea service. Until quite recently, some boys entered certain pre-sea schools at ages of between twelve and thirteen; the courses for these boys being of three or four years' duration. Today, boys are recruited at sixteen and upwards and their pre-sea courses are of four terms or less. This means that these older boys are able to pursue their normal general education for a longer period than those who were recruited at twelve or thirteen. All this makes sense, for a boy who wants to go to sea should be allowed to do so soon after he leaves his secondary school and then be taught the bulk of the theoretical knowledge he requires only after he has become familiar with ships and their routines.

The few remaining cadet training ships in the Merchant Navy provide an interesting alternative pattern of training. Here a larger number of cadets than is usual is carried on a normal, working, cargo ship. They may be carried either, as in the New Zealand Shipping Company's *Otaio* and *Rakaia*, as a working crew, or, as with the training units of Cayzer, Irvine & Co., British India Steam Navigation Company, and Elder Dempster, quite additional to a full ship's company. In all cases, instructional staff and training facilities are provided on board. These ships together train some 10 per cent of the total deck cadet intake in the Merchant Navy. Their principle is excellent, since they actively pursue a boy's training throughout his apprenticeship, instead of leaving him for long periods to the vagaries of a correspondence course. Unlike nautical colleges, these ships receive no form of central financial support, but this, one hopes, will be remedied with the application of the Industrial Training Act to the shipping industry. The only specially built cadet ship is the *Otaio*, all the others being cargo ships which have suitable accommodation. It seems doubtful that this form of training will persist, which is a pity.

Of late there have been considerable efforts to standardize the entry qualifications for deck cadets. The present nominal minimum level is three passes at the Ordinary Level of the General Certificate of Education (or Certificate of Secondary Education, Grade 1). These should include mathematics, English, and a science subject. The standard is open to criticism in both directions. On the one hand, it is hard today to get enough boys to go to sea, and many are accepted without reaching the required standard. This overloads them, as they work at sea by correspondence to obtain the needed passes. On the other hand, the shipping industry requires a certain percentage of its intake to be boys of higher academic ability, say of "A"-level standard. These boys, and their advisers, are not likely to be attracted to a career with a minimum entry standard well below their attainments, and where promotion is apparently largely independent of ability.

A recent development in the training of deck cadets is the institution of Ordinary National Diploma courses in Nautical Science. The entry requirements for these courses are four appropriate "O"-level passes, and the course is an industry-based sandwich one, over the period of the apprenticeship. In common with other recognized schemes of training, successful completion of the O.N.D. carries remission of the sea time necessary before a student can attempt the Board of Trade Second Mate's certificate. The student obtaining an Ordinary National Diploma is also exempted from some parts of the Second and First Mate's certificates.

Engineer cadets

There are about 3300 engineer cadets at all stages of their training in the Merchant Navy. They undergo a $4\frac{1}{2}$-year phased training scheme, leading to an Ordinary National Diploma in Engineering. Between 700 and 800 boys enter upon the course each year. This training scheme was instituted in 1952 to help overcome a chronic shortage of qualified engineers at sea. The success of the scheme is indicated by the fact that of the 17,624 uncertificated engineers at sea today, 700 are ex-engineer cadets obtaining the necessary watchkeeping service to obtain a Second Class certificate. Thus, *pro rata*, the cadets obtain about $2\frac{1}{2}$ times as many certificates as do the traditionally trained engineers.

The engineer cadets' course normally starts with a two-year Phase I in a college ashore, sponsored by the employing shipping company. At the end of this period the boys go to sea for the 18 months of Phase II, and then return to college for Phase III. Thus the pattern is very different from that on the deck side, which is moving away from the very long pre-sea courses.

The long pre-sea course is open to criticism, as a boy joining a shipping company is likely to be keen to get to sea as soon as possible and may be discouraged if he cannot do so. One scheme that overcomes this problem is the cadet ship *Otaio*, referred to above. She carries up to 40 Phase I engineer cadets as well as the deck cadets. They are provided with a classroom, laboratory and workshop, and three qualified instructors, not necessarily seafarers, are carried. The cadets are entirely additional to a full engine room complement. This scheme has produced some very good results, not least of which has been the friendship engendered between the two groups of deck and engineer cadets. This friendship and mutual understanding continues when they return as officers, and has done much to improve inter-departmental relationship within that company. The same principle has been followed by those nautical colleges which train deck and engineer cadets alongside each other.

The continuing shortage of qualified marine engineers has resulted in other schemes being instituted, similarly organized to the Ordinary National Diploma courses, but leading to an Ordinary National Certificate, or to Part A of the Second Class Engineer's certificate.

Radio cadets

There are no radio cadets at sea, as all radio officers in the Merchant Navy have obtained at least the Postmaster General's Second Class certificate, and may have obtained the First Class certificate, before coming to sea. Several marine radio colleges train these boys for sea and, at the present time, there are about 1000 students in training. The course is of about two years' duration, the length depending on how far the student proceeds before going to sea. The trend is for an increasing number of radio officers to come to sea fully qualified, and many also obtain a City and Guilds of London Institute Telecommunications certificate, at Intermediate or Final level.

Purser and catering cadets

The numbers of these are extremely small, as the vast majority of officers in the catering department are drawn from ratings of that department. The requirements for Purser and catering officer vary considerably between different trades and companies. Training for these positions is highly specialized and is peculiar to the company or group concerned. Training is normally carried on within the company, although at least one nautical catering college runs, in addition to many other shorter courses, a three-year sandwich course for catering cadets. This is run in close co-operation with the employing shipping company. During the course the students take the certificate of competency as ship's cook, as well as two appropriate examinations of the City and Guilds of London Institute.

Officers

Until very recently, the only qualifications obtained by ship's officers of the two main departments were Board of Trade certificates of competency. To attempt the examinations for these certificates a seafarer must have reached a certain age, have satisfactory eyesight, and have served a certain length of time in an appropriate capacity at sea. Additionally, candidates for engineers' certificates must have served an appropriate apprenticeship, and candidates for deck certificates must obtain a first aid certificate and a radar observer's certificate. The first aid certificate syllabus is being revised to bring it more in line with the needs of persons dealing with disease and injury on board ship. Thus, on the deck side, three weeks' attendance at a radar observer's course represents the only compulsory schooling that an officer must have between coming to sea and obtaining command. The engineer need never attend school after finishing his apprenticeship.

In spite of this, nautical and marine engineering colleges flourish and proliferate, with men arriving to start studying on each day of each week throughout the year, and with examinations held at fortnightly intervals. It is small wonder that nautical professional qualifications hardly enjoy parity of esteem with corresponding qualifications ashore.

The syllabuses for Board of Trade certificates have also been targets for much criticism. It can be argued that the content of the Master's certificate does little to prepare a man to command a ship. Similarly some engineer's papers, particularly that in Engineering Knowledge, have little relevance to marine engineering as it is practised at sea today.

There would seem to be a case for a radical reappraisal of the parts played by the colleges and the Board of Trade respectively, in the certification of marine personnel. Courses of stated length, with regular entry, and largely internally examined with external moderation, might provide a better system.

The introduction of Ordinary National Diploma courses for

cadets marks the first step in a ladder of worthwhile professional qualifications for seafarers. On the deck side, the O.N.D. is complemented by the degree of Bachelor of Science in Nautical Studies; the course for this is a $4\frac{1}{2}$-year industry-based sandwich. On the engineering side, the way is open to a Higher National Diploma, and a B.Sc. in Marine Engineering. Some of the proposals for courses leading to the B.Sc. in Nautical Studies have been phrased so as to admit students from the engineering and business side of the industry, but it seems unlikely that this degree will interest the man wanting to pursue one particular subject in depth. It is however, of great value to men wanting to broaden the scope of their knowledge of ships and the sea.

Electrical officers at sea have needed no professional qualifications. It is now suggested that they should aim at an Ordinary National Certificate in Electrical Engineering, or an Electrical Technician's certificate.

The examination and qualification of radio officers is the preserve of the Postmaster General as far as telecommunications is concerned, and of the Board of Trade for the Radar Maintenance certificate. There may be some rationalization of certificates here, to match the changing demands on the radio officer at sea.

Catering officers are almost all recruited from ratings, on the basis of individual ability and potential. There is no requirement for statutory certification, apart from the carriage of a certificated ship's cook on board.

A group that is not statistically significant, but which exerts considerable influence in training, is that of the companies' training staff. Where such staff are carried on board, with explicit instructional duties, it would seem reasonable that they should receive training in teaching theory and techniques.

Deck officers

The pattern of examinations for Board of Trade certificates of competency as deck officers has remained basically unchanged for some years. There are 12,546 certificated and 1414 uncertificated Masters and deck officers in the Merchant Navy. In 1966, 865 Second Mate's, 725 Mate's, 504 Master's and 16 Extra Master's certificates of competency were granted. There has been a steady decline in the number of Extra Masters, from the 32 passes of 1964. This is probably due, in large part, to the inception of degree courses in nautical subjects, which are discussed below. The difference in numbers between those passing for Second Mate and for Master is a measure of the loss of trained men from active seafaring. To obtain an accurate current picture of this wastage, it is necessary to compare the numbers of Second Mates for a given year with the number of Masters two to three years later, but the figures would not be markedly different from those given here. Comparatively few of these lost men remain within the shipping industry ashore.

Under the aegis of the Council for National Academic Awards, courses leading to the degree of Bachelor of Science (Nautical Studies) have started at the Plymouth and Liverpool nautical colleges, and some others are awaiting approval. Two nautical colleges, at Cardiff and Warsash, belong to institutions which are degree-granting in their own right. Cardiff offers a nautical degree of the University of Wales, while Warsash has instituted a course for a nautical degree of Southampton University.

All these degree courses are four- to five-year sandwich courses. The details vary between colleges, but in general it can be said that entry requirements correspond to those of other university courses, either G.C.E. passes, a good pass at the Ordinary National Diploma, or a First Mate's certificate, in conjunction with certain G.C.E. passes. Initially, some colleges are offering "straight-through" courses for suitable students already holding a Master's certificate. This puts the degree within the reach of men in their mid to late twenties, who have already obtained their full professional qualifications. In some cases, courses may be offered to persons from all sections of shipping, with choices of subjects designed to allow students to remain broadly within their own fields.

These maritime graduates, and there may be up to 100 of them per year when all the courses are established, should have a significant impact on thinking within the shipping industry. An interesting development that remains to be explored is the possibility of nautical students registering with the C.N.A.A. as postgraduate research students, for programmes of research leading to higher degrees. At the time of writing no nautical men have done this, but there would seem to be no reason why a suitable proposal should not receive the Council's approval.

Another development in officer training has been the growth of short specialized courses, mainly for senior officers. Attendance on many of these is not restricted to deck officers, but it is convenient to discuss these courses here. Radar courses, both simulator and observer, and gyro maintenance courses, have been held for some time to fulfil specific needs. A radar observer's course is now obligatory before a Second Mate's certificate can be obtained, and it is reasonable to presume that the radar simulator course will one day become a pre-requisite to the granting of a Master's certificate. Gyro maintenance courses cater for officers who, with an elementary knowledge of electricity and machinery, are called upon to keep the ship's gyro compass continually in running order. In passing, it could be mentioned that a suitable adaptation of the radar maintenance course could perform a similar valuable function where, as still occurs, a deck officer is called upon to maintain radar equipment.

More recently instituted short courses deal with the refreshing and updating of officer's knowledge, of safety, man management and personnel relations, cargo gear, and work study. The British Shipping Federation instituted its own peripatetic courses in management and personnel relations in 1964 and over 1000 officers have attended the 50 courses held up to 1967. The Honourable Company of Master Mariners holds a biennial conference of senior officers. Some nautical colleges run similar courses, the best known being those at Plymouth, and many of the more progressive shipping companies hold them for their own men. Any estimate of the numbers of men attending such courses could only be a wild guess, but since there are over 40,000 officers, of all departments, in the Merchant Navy, there is plenty of scope in the field. It could be argued that an officer should attend such a course say every five years, in which case at least 8000 places would be required each year.

Engineer officers

There are 5829 certificated and 17,624 uncertificated engineer officers in the Merchant Navy. In 1966, 430 Second Class, 346 First Class, and 14 Extra First Class Engineers' certificates were granted. The pattern of Board of Trade examinations for engineer officers is similar to that for deck officers, except that engineers have to obtain two certificates, as opposed to the Mates' three. A deck officer has a reasonable chance of obtaining his certificates within the normal period of paid study leave, but the engineer officer has not. The big difference between the departments is in the ratio of certificated to uncertificated officer personnel. This ratio is about 9:1 in favour of certificated personnel for deck officers, but about 1:3 for engineers. The success of the alternative training scheme, replacing, as it does, an apprenticeship served in heavy engineering ashore with an apprenticeship in the shipping industry, indicates that an ever increasing proportion of seagoing engineers will be found from this source, and that the traditional method of entry will decline in importance. This will gradually alter the above ratio, and will increase the proportion of qualified engineer officers at sea.

The investment in this alternative form of training is considerable, and the shipowner will want to be very sure that the results, in terms of certificated engineers staying at sea, to justify the scheme economically. While the standard of the seagoing engineer has undoubtedly been improved, it remains to be seen whether some other incentive, perhaps a gratuity paid after a given period of service, will be needed to keep these men at sea.

A small number of O.N.D. engineer cadets proceed on to Higher National Diploma courses in Mechanical Engineering.

The numbers are not significant, and it is possible that losses of these men will be considerable. These students have ample opportunity, during their time ashore, to evaluate their prospects both within and without the shipping industry. There are also courses available, at the universities of Surrey and Newcastle, leading to the degree of B.Sc. in Marine Engineering. Again, the numbers of students are so small, at the moment, as to be insignificant.

Radio officers

There are 3175 radio officers in the Merchant Navy, and most of these are fully qualified, with a First Class P.M.G. certificate and a B.O.T. Radar Maintenance certificate.

With the increasing use being made of the radio telephone, the practical telecommunications part of a radio officer's job has declined in importance relative to electronics and maintenance. Thus the radio officer may, one day, be redefined as an electronics officer, and it would not seem unreasonable for his watchkeeping and maintenance functions to be combined with those of one or both of the other major departments.

Improved qualifications for an "electronics officer" might result in only one P.M.G. certificate, and a parallel O.N.D./H.N.D. scheme, which, combined with experience on the job, should result in highly competent and versatile men.

There is one interesting anomaly concerning the work of radio officers, which arises occasionally. For historical and other reasons some shipping companies do not employ their radio officers directly, but hire these officers from a marine radio company. Now and then, when the ship's radar set is not supplied by the company which employs the radio officer, it falls to the deck department to maintain this radar set. This is done despite the fact that very few deck officers are competent to tackle this work, and that the radio officer may possess a radar maintenance certificate, albeit obtained with a different make of equipment. Good relations aboard ship generally result in effective maintenance of the ship's equipment in these circumstances, but the existence of the situation is clearly an undesirable anomaly.

Catering officers

The Registrar General of Shipping and Seamen does not publish separate figures for the numbers of officers and ratings in the catering department, but of the 30,875 personnel in this department it is probable that 3000–4000 are officers. As has been stated, the requirements for advancement to officer rank in the catering department consist largely of personal ability and aptitude. Three week courses are run for Chief Stewards of non-passenger ships, with the emphasis on those aspects of the Chief Steward's job that are novel to men working up from the position of ship's cook or Second Steward.

In large passenger ships, where the catering department is of paramount importance to the ship's economics, the officers of this department are very carefully selected and trained internally in Company procedures and practice.

Ratings

A visit to a boy ratings' training school today would open the eyes of many a salty Mate, accustomed to fulminate over the deficiencies of his crew. The largest of the training schools is that run by the National Sea Training Trust at Gravesend, where deck and catering boys are trained before they go to sea. There are many others up and down the country, some of them with origins well back into the last century. It seemed desirable to our forefathers both to care for destitute boys of good character, and to cope with young offenders, by training them for a career at sea. Thus the *Arethusa*, the last ship to go into action entirely under sail, was secured by Lord Shaftesbury for boys in the former category in 1874. Most of the ships have gone now, but the schools remain, some administered by the Home Office, some privately, and the largest, as has been stated, by the shipping industry. No longer are young offenders encouraged to go to sea; the Shipping Federation ensures that only boys of the highest character are recruited into the Merchant Navy.

There are similar short pre-sea courses for engine room ratings, and a number of companies, which are experimenting with teams of "dual-purpose" ratings on some ships, are training their own men for this purpose.

Deck ratings

There are 23,531 in the Merchant Navy. Most of these have been trained at one of the Shipping Federation's schools, where they attend a twelve-week course to give them the rudiments of their craft. It may be noted here that these boys are taught far more than most of them will be allowed to use on board, and there is perhaps room to look critically at the function of the junior rating on board. Obviously somebody must be employed to perform the menial tasks, but there are many ways in which a deck boy could make better use of all he learns before coming to sea.

A deck rating requires to obtain a lifeboat efficiency certificate and an efficient deck hand's certificate. With these, and after three years' sea service, he is rated as Able Bodied Seaman. Thereafter, his promotion to Boatswain is entirely dependent on himself and his employers, and in most cases prospective petty officers will receive no instruction at all on aspects of supervisory duties. A few shipping companies are doing something about this problem and in 1967 the Shipping Federation introduced "Supervisors' Courses" for these petty officers.

Figures quoted above show that in 1966 only about 2 per cent of the Second Mate's certificates were awarded to ratings. This is in marked contrast to the situation prevailing in the United States, and in some countries of Europe. In our Merchant Navy, a rating who aspires to certificated rank works under appalling disadvantages. In most cases he must start learning entirely unfamiliar subject matter by correspondence, a method which, although an integral and essential part of Merchant Naval training, is not remarkable for its efficiency, nor for its ability to maintain students' motivation. The nautical colleges and the Seafarers' Education Service provide all possible help, but those few ratings who persevere with study at sea and achieve their end deserve every credit. As a result of the recommendations of the Pearson Committee there may be a move to improve the circumstances under which ratings study for professional certificates, and the report of the Seafarers' Education Service's Research Officer contains information that could be used to improve the ship as a place in which to learn. Ratings should be among the first to benefit from any implementation of these reports.

Engine room ratings

Much of what has been said above of deck ratings applies with equal force to those in the engine room. The major stumbling block in the way of the engine room rating who wishes to become a certificated engineer is the necessity of obtaining workshop experience. A two-year course running at Leith Nautical College provides this experience, although to date, of the 9937 engine room ratings in the Merchant Navy, the number rising to officer rank is not significant.

Catering ratings

The catering department contains 30,875 men all told, and about 26,000 of these are probably ratings. A ship must carry a certificated cook, and the normal source of officers for this department is from the ratings.

The Shipping Federation's school at Gravesend provides an eight-week pre-sea course for catering boys, at the end of which they go to sea as either galley boys or steward's boys. As with the deck department, these boys reach a very good standard before going to sea, and must experience some disillusion with their role on board at first. To help these boys to continue their studies when they get to sea, a correspondence course is being devised by staff of the North-West Kent College of Technology, and run in conjunction with the Seafarers' Education Service, in English and arithmetic. The numbers who persevere with this course are likely to be few; the course will give them a good background, which should enable them to progress in their chosen career without the difficulties often experienced by those who return to book learning after a prolonged absence.

There are other, longer courses available for prospective cooks and stewards notably at the Liverpool Nautical Catering College. Many of these courses are for men already at sea who wish to specialize in a particular aspect of their craft. The ship's cook course now lasts twelve weeks. The course and examination are open to all who have been to sea for a month, although it is normal practice for a man to be about a year at sea before attending. Thereafter there are refresher and advanced cookery courses, while other courses cover bakery, confectionery, and advanced waiting.

Non-vocational education

The College of the Sea, a department of the Seafarers' Education Service, plays by far the major role in the non-vocational education for seafarers. While correspondence courses play a part in professional nautical education, students for Board of Trade certificates invariably attend a nautical college before attempting their examinations. For most non-vocational work the correspondence course, or correspondence tutorial, is the sole method open to seafarers. The College of the Sea enrols about 500 students per year, on a very wide range of courses. At any one time, about 1000 men or about 1 per cent of the Merchant Navy population, are enrolled on a course with the College of the Sea. It is probable that about another 100–200 are enrolled with other correspondence colleges, principally for such examinations as those of the Institute of Transport. About half the College of the Sea students are studying mathematics, about a third English, and the others are spread over a wide variety of subjects, ranging from geography and economics to art and languages.

The methods adopted by the College of the Sea are extremely elastic, and enable courses to be designed to suit each student. A very large number of people give their services to the College as voluntary tutors, and thus each tutor deals only with a small number of students. This enables an individual, personal link to be developed between tutor and student.

Returns from College of the Sea courses are no better than from other correspondence courses, afloat or ashore, but judged by seafarers' G.C.E. results, students who persevere in a course achieve significantly better results than those who attempt to study on their own.

A breakdown by departments of the active students enrolled with the College of the Sea indicates that, *pro rata*, the deck department, excluding radio officers, provides five times the proportion of students than does the engine room department, and four times the proportion from the catering department. Further, a "studiousness index" can be calculated for each group, defined as the ratio:

$$\frac{\text{The group as a percentage of the total Merchant Navy population}}{\text{Number of College of the Sea students from this group, expressed as a percentage of the total number of students}}$$

This ratio, for groups as listed by the Registrar General of Shipping and Seamen, is as follows:

Deck cadets	4·78	Deck ratings	0·97	Catering dept.	0·43
Radio officers	3·28	Miscellaneous	0·91	E.R. ratings	0·39
Masters and deck officers	2·23	Engineer cadets	0·90	Engineer officers	0·36

These groupings reflect incentive to study—some deck cadets need to obtain further G.C.E. passes; suitable conditions for study—radio and deck officers are most favoured here; and the fact that hard physical labour on the job, in the engineering and catering departments, does not leave much energy for active study in leisure time.

With so few students aboard any one ship—the 1000 students are spread over the Merchant Navy, in about 1600 foreign-going and 700 home-trade ships—it is expensive to provide any learning aids on board for the students' use. Some experimenting has taken place with the use of programmed learning and teaching machines on board ship, and an artist-tutor is currently spending his second peripatetic year in merchant ships. The most important aids for the solitary student will probably continue to be a worthwhile technical library on board, and tutorial help by correspondence, using air mail. These can be supported wherever possible by the use of learning aids and peripatetic lectures, but these are likely to remain uneconomic.

Conclusion

Throughout vocational nautical education the trends are toward integrated, phased systems of training, with the industrial phases used to revise and consolidate work initially done ashore. As numbers of men decline, both aboard individual ships, and in the industry as a whole, it becomes more important to ensure that each one is properly trained to carry out his job effectively.

Also, it could be argued, that the sea is a job for young, single men, that the industry must accept high wastage rates, and that both the shipping industry and the government have an obligation to ensure that the men coming ashore are fitted for a change in their careers. Certainly, as many as possible of the men leaving the sea should be absorbed into the shipping industry ashore, where their experience will not be wasted. The nautical degree courses will be a source of qualified men for all branches of the industry but any suggestions that seafarers should be prepared, by the shipping industry, for careers not related to shipping should be accompanied by proposals for State finance. An industry, whose training costs have been put at £4 million (or $3\frac{1}{2}$ per cent of the wage bill), is unlikely to want to invest more money in training men to leave the sea; even though such training may increase the well-being of seafarers.

The introduction of dual-purpose ratings has paved the way to smaller crews, and to more efficient operation and maintenance of ships. There has been little inclination, as yet, to think in terms of dual-purpose officers. Perhaps the length of training that might be required is a deterrent. The United States Federal Maritime Academy started training a number of students, about ten per cent of their intake, for this role in 1965. These will complete their course in 1969, when they should obtain a degree in nautical science from the academy, and also be eligible to sit for both Mate's and engineer's licences. Clearly it is too soon to estimate the value of such a scheme. A French experiment, which set out to train established officers of each department in the techniques of the other, has been abandoned.

A notable omission on the nautical education scene is that of a professional Institute that would work to raise the standard of the profession by the use of examinations for degrees of membership. The Institute of Navigation appears to have declined this role, but an opportunity may, at some time, occur for an amalgamation of deck interests with the seagoing part of the Institute of Marine Engineers in order to create an Institute of Shipping that could be representative of all seafarers aspiring to professional standards.

On the training side, the possibility of an Industrial Training Board for the shipping industry is of interest. Such a Board, if established, would perform many of the functions of the present Merchant Navy Training Board, but, in addition, it would have power to take a training levy from companies within the industry, and to give grants to those carrying out satisfactory training programmes. Thus it would control funds that would enable it to develop training within the industry as it considered necessary.

This brief survey has done no more than outline the various training schemes as they exist today. Any seafarer will be able to fill in the picture for his own department, but many may find something of interest in the overall view here presented.

CHAPTER 12

Work Study

by S. STARKS

WORK study, these days, is almost respectable: there have been so many successful applications that, for the most part, it is recognized as a very valuable management service. Of course, most people say that work study cannot be applied to their jobs and only welcome its introduction when it affects someone else. This is understandable when you consider that the aim of any work study investigator is to find a more effective way of working and consequently, whenever it is employed, it implies that the existing methods may be inefficient. Naturally the implication is resented by those who are supervising or employed on the job to be studied, even though they were not initially responsible for establishing the methods in use. Successful work study will only be possible if this problem is recognized, appreciated and over-come jointly by the investigators and the management. It is important that when this has been achieved, the intention to co-operate should be made apparent and communicated to everyone who is likely to be involved. Some part of the difficulty is almost certainly due to lack of understanding of the subject itself and, consequently, in this chapter I shall try to explain the basic principles and illustrate a few of the more appropriate techniques. The use of slick "before" and "after" examples from other industries will be avoided as these often only reinforce the opinion that work study is limited in application to repetitive-type work.

Work study really embraces two closely related subjects:

method study and work measurement. The study of methods will probably be the more rewarding of the two in the shipping industry, but a knowledge of ways of estimating time may be useful in some circumstances. Logically, the time that work is going to take cannot be determined until a standard method has been established, and, consequently, the principles and techniques of method study are usually presented before those of work measurement.

Method study

Short articles and lectures on method study are usually illustrated by impressive examples from manufacturing industries and this sometimes leads to confusion between the basic analytical approach to method improvement and the recording techniques which may be used as aids to method analysis. It is the analysis and critical examination which are common to investigation in all types of industry and, in applying these, the observer will follow a set procedure regardless of the nature of the work. His first task is to observe the work in some detail. For example, he would not accept an overall description of a job like "Discharge timber and stack on wharf", but would establish the individual activities which go to make up the job:

Timber loaded onto sling;
Transported by crane to trailer on dockside;
Loaded onto trailer;
Quantity and type checked against bill of lading;
Transported on trailer to stacking area;
Removed from trailer by fork-lift truck;
Transported to stack;
Stacked.

Wherever possible this information is obtained by direct observation on the grounds that what "is done" often differs substantially from what "is thought to be done". Next, the observer will subject any key activities in the sequence to a series of questions. The first of these is to determine the *purpose* of the operation. Strange as it may sound, there are occasions when jobs can be completely eliminated. I will resist the temptation to quote slick examples as these are largely irrelevant to the shipping world, but you may like to consider whether, in the above example, there was any real necessity to load the timber onto the trailer for transportation to the stacking area. Elimination of work is, by far, the most rewarding aspect of method study but, obviously, this is not always possible. Subsequent questioning of the activities cover the *place* where the work is carried out and consideration is given to alternative locations which may be used to advantage. Similarly, thought about the *person* or persons carrying out the work may give rise to ideas resulting in change of grade of labour, more even distribution of work load and better utilization of manpower. Demarcation may raise problems here but productivity agreements can sometimes be used to overcome them. The *sequence* of activities is also studied to see whether changes might reduce waiting time or to permit operations to be performed simultaneously. Finally, the *means* of performing the job will be studied. This usually relates to equipment or lack of it and to the development of machinery or tools which would make more effective use of effort.

The examination of activities is never haphazard. Frequently answers to the questions are written on specially designed forms to ensure that all possible alternatives are considered.

Even with a critical examination sheet, it would be difficult to carry out the analysis of a work pattern unless the activity sequence has been clearly presented. Thus the work study observer uses a series of recording techniques which have been designed to present a process or procedure in a simple but concise form. Not all recording techniques are suitable for all situations; some have been designed specifically for highly repetitive, short cycle work and may entail the use of a cine camera. Obviously these will not be of any value for the normal day to day operations aboard ships, but the rejection of a particular recording technique should not be used as a reason for rejecting method study as a whole.

CRITICAL EXAMINATION SHEET

The present facts		Alternatives	Selected alternatives
Purpose What is achieved?	Is it necessary? Why?	What else could done?	What should be done?
Place Where is it done?	Why there?	Where else could it be done?	Where should it be done?
Person Who does it?	Why that person?	Who else could do it?	Who should do it?
Sequence When is it done? Before: After:	Why then?	When else could it be done?	When should it be done?
Means How is it done?	Why that way?	How else could it be done?	How should it be done?

One of the most useful and versatile of the recording techniques which would have applications in both the technical and clerical aspects of shipping is the Flow Process Chart. It uses five symbols to represent the different activities:

○ Operation	▷ Transport
□ Inspection	D Delay

▽ Storage

Using these symbols to present the off-loading of the timber mentioned earlier in this chapter, we would get a Flow Process Chart.

Subject: Material (Timber)

Operation: Off-loading timber and stacking on wharf.

Symbol	Description	Remarks
▽	In hold	
①	Loaded onto sling	
▷	To trailer on dockside	Crane
②	Loaded onto trailer	
☐	Checked against bill of lading	
▷	Await completion of load	2 slings per trailer
▷	To stacking area	Tractor and trailer
③	Off-loaded	Fork lift
▷	To stack	Fork lift
④	Stacked	Fork lift
▽	In stack	

This chart could be supplemented by a drawing of the working area with symbols superimposed to show the relative positions of the areas where the various activities are performed (Fig. 12.1).

Flow Diagram

Subject: Material (Timber)

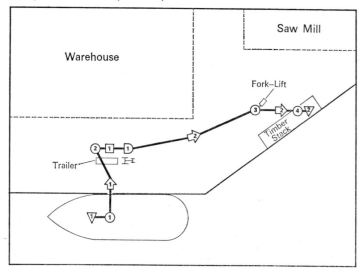

FIG. 12.1. Flow diagram for timber moving from ship's hold to stack on wharf.

The flow diagram, as this drawing is called, only shows the symbols and, consequently, it is usually used in conjunction with the Flow Process Chart. In this example, the material (timber) has been taken as the subject of the chart; but, if the study warranted, the activities of a man could have been recorded just as easily.

Where a group of men or men and machines are employed, it may be advantageous to show their activities relative to each other against a time scale. This can be done quite effectively on a Gantt-type chart which is usually referred to as a Multiple Activity Chart (Fig. 12.2).

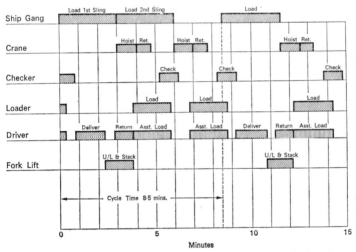

FIG. 12.2. Multiple Activity Chart showing the operations during the movement of the timber from the ship's hold to the stack on the wharf.

The charts I have illustrated are, of course, not the only ones available to the work study practitioner but they should be sufficient to show the place of recording techniques in method study procedures.

Charts, then, are the tools which help in carrying out the analysis. The next thing to decide is where to start. Jobs are not just picked at random. Generally one would look for those jobs with high labour cost or high labour content; the principle being that such jobs offer the greatest potential saving. Alternatively a job may be chosen because it tends to create a "bottleneck" in the sense that its completion controls the commencement of other work. Perhaps the best guidance I can give on selection of jobs to be studied is to point out that the carrying out of a study costs time and money and, unless the potential saving will more than compensate for the expenditure of both, the study can serve no purpose.

Finally, the changes in method which have been developed and approved by management have to be introduced, and this is the time when a great deal of tact and patience is necessary. Success will depend largely on the atmosphere which was created at the start of the investigation and on the extent to which people doing the work were consulted during the study. The important thing to remember is that time spent on explanation and discussion of the reasons for change is never wasted; haste at this stage will often result in failure.

I have presented the stages in a method study investigation in what appears to me to be the best order for explanation. To summarize, here are the steps in their correct chronological sequence:

Select   the work to be studied,
Record   the present method,
Examine critically, and
Develop the best method under the existing circumstances.
Install   and maintain the new method.

Work measurement

Most managers would find it extremely difficult to manage without some knowledge of the times required by the process for which they are responsible. Without a knowledge of these times it would be virtually impossible to plan, cost, provide effective manning or even navigate a ship. In many cases, the more accurate the measurement the more effective the management.

Work measurement is a collective term covering a series of techniques for establishing the time taken to do manual tasks. The techniques include time study, analytical estimating, predetermined motion–time systems, and activity sampling. However, the last three all include some basic time study principles so their acceptance demands some appreciation of these principles.

There are two factors which will influence the time taken to complete any given job. The first is the method used and the second is the speed and effectiveness of working. Methods can be controlled fairly easily by issuing instructions, and attempts to time jobs before this has been done are likely to be futile. Furthermore a time is valueless to management unless it is related to some norm or standard of performance. In work study, this standard performance is defined as: "The pace at which a normally qualified operative will work provided he is motivated to perform his task."

This is a fairly brisk pace and is sometimes said to be represented by a man of average build walking on level ground at four miles per hour.

Work study personnel are trained to recognize this and other levels of performance over a fairly wide range of activities and to express their ratings on a numerical scale. (See p. 174.)

A practical time study observer will usually be competent to judge performance within $\pm$ 5 points on the scale.

Thus, when timing a job, the observer will record not only the watch or clock time but also his estimate of the performance of the rate of working. Then, by elementary arithmetic, he is able to convert the recorded time to basic time using the simple formula:

$$\text{Basic time} = \frac{\text{Observed time} \times \text{rating}}{\text{standard rating}}.$$

For example, a job which took 15 minutes when the rate of working was assessed at 80 would give a basic time of $\dfrac{15 \times 80}{100} = 12$ minutes.

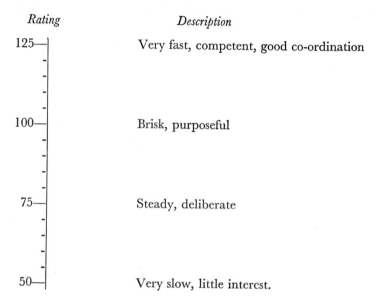

Rating	Description
125—	Very fast, competent, good co-ordination
100—	Brisk, purposeful
75—	Steady, deliberate
50—	Very slow, little interest.

Expressing time values at standard performance is fairly common, but where operatives are not expected to achieve this level, perhaps through lack of motivation, it might be advisable to increase the values by setting them at, say, 75 or 80. This is done quite easily by substituting the selected performance level for the standard rating in the formula above.

Rating assessment is made quite independently of the timing and in practice, although the results for the two occasions should be approximately the same, they may not be identical as they are in the example. There are further refinements in actually taking a time study. For example, the job will probably be broken down into elements which will be timed and rated individually; whenever possible, the observer will take times over several cycles and take an average of the basic times for each element before totalling them to get the basic time for the whole job.

You will probably have noticed that I am using the term "basic time" and not "standard time". This is because the value is not complete until certain allowances have been added. The first of these is the rest or fatigue allowance; a percentage is added to the basic time to compensate for the effort, temperature and other factors which are likely to affect the time taken for working under different conditions. Various tables have been drawn up giving recommended values for the different factors, but these have often been designed for a particular industry and, in all probability, the shipping industry, because of its widely differing conditions, will develop one of its own.

I had intended that this chapter should be very general and as far as possible would exclude references and examples relating to manufacturing industries. However there is one incident I will quote to make my next point.

I had been discussing with a bay manager the advantages of having time values for all the operations in his section. Costing would be simple, manning and planning would be more effective, and output would probably be increased by introducing an incentive scheme. All this he agreed with and then commented, "But what about last week when the flywheel came off that press and nearly injured someone? How would you time that?"

Of course allowance must be made for likely contingencies but these cannot be expected to include disasters. So standard time for a job is really basic time+rest allowance+contingency allowances.

One way of establishing the contingency allowance is to use one of the remaining work measurement techniques: activity sampling.

This is a statistical technique and uses the principle that the values obtained from samples can be used as estimates of the corresponding values for the whole. Taking a very simple example, suppose we wanted to know what proportion of time a group of men spent working as opposed to not working. This could, of course, be determined by continuous observations and recording the times for each of the activities; but this would be costly and time consuming. The alternative is to do this by sampling. Random times for observation are pre-determined to cover the working period. Subsequently, at each of these times, the observer records, at the instant of observation, the number of men working. This is usually done using a tally system:

Activity	Tally	Total	%
Working	/////////////////////////	360	60
Not working	////////////	240	40

The indication from this example is that the utilization of the group is 60 per cent. But all samples are liable to error, so how confident can we be that the answer is reliable? Again statistical theory will help with a fairly simple formula giving us the limits of reliability.

$$\text{Limits of reliability} = \pm 2 \sqrt{\frac{p \times q}{n}},$$

where p=percentage observations on selected activities,
q=percentage observations on other activities, or $(100-p)$,
n=number of observations.

$$\text{Limits} = \pm 2 \sqrt{\frac{60 \times 40}{600}} = 2 \sqrt{4} = 4.$$

So, with reasonable confidence (95 per cent), we can say that the utilization is 60 ± 4 per cent or that the true result probably lies between 56 and 64 per cent.

This technique can easily be extended to determine contingency allowances if the working and not working sections are broken down into clearly defined activities; for example, awaiting instructions, collecting materials, unserviceable equipment, etc.

A further development of the sampling technique is its use as a means of determining times, and it is particularly useful when dealing with groups of men as it enables a number of values to be established simultaneously. The following table lists the activities of the men and equipment taking part in our earlier example of off-loading the timber:

Off-Load Timber and Stack on Wharf

Start	Finish	Elapsed, min
0900	1225	205
1300	1640	220
Total		425

Number of loads stacked = 50
Time per load = 8·5 min

Group/ (1) equipment	Activity (2)	No. of (3) observations	% (4)	Total (5) time	Time (6) for cycle	Time (7) per element
Ship gang	Load sling	282	70·5	300	6·0	3·0
	Wait	118:400	29·5	125	2·5	
Crane	Timber to dock	94	23·5	100	2·0	1·0
	Return	70	17·5	75	1·5	0·75
	Wait	236:400	59·0	250	5·0	/////////
Checker	Check	94	23·5	100	2·0	1·0
	Wait	306:400	76·5	325	6·5	/////////
Loader	Load	188	47·0	200	4·0	2·0
	Wait	212:400	53·0	225	4·5	/////////
Driver	Assist loader	188	47·0	200	4·0	2·0
	Deliver	70	17·5	75	1·5	1·5
	Return	48	12·0	50	1·0	1·0
	Wait	94:400	23·5	100	2·0	/////////
Fork lift	Stack timber	70	17·5	75	1·5	1·5
	Wait	330:400	82·5	350	7·0	/////////

You will notice that, in addition to recording the number of observations on each activity, the elapsed time and the number of loads have also been noted. Thus, in column (5) the percentages have been converted to total time spent on each operation and, in column (6), these are expressed as time per cycle. Finally, element times are determined taking into account the frequency with which they occur in each cycle. For example, the cycle time for loading the sling is 6 minutes, but as this is performed twice for each load of timber stacked then the time to load the sling is 3 minutes. Notice, too, it would have been possible to introduce a rating factor into the study either by estimating the overall performance for each manual group or, alternatively, by taking an average of sample ratings made during the course of the study.

To illustrate this point, suppose the loader and the driver had carried out the loading at an estimated performance of 80. Then the time taken for each cycle could have been converted to basic time:

$$\text{Basic time} = \frac{4 \cdot 0 \times 80}{100} = 3 \cdot 2 \text{ minutes per cycle,}$$

giving an element time of $1 \cdot 6$ minutes instead of $2 \cdot 0$ minutes.

Activity sampling provides a very convenient method of collecting times for Multiple Activity Charts where the value for individual elements are necessary for the analysis and development of alternative methods requiring change of sequence or re-allocation of the work load.

You will be aware by this time that all the examples in this chapter are related to one job. Certain information like distances, wage rates and grades of labour, depreciation and hire charges on equipment have been omitted so you will not be able to solve the problem completely. However, I would suggest that you review the procedure in the light of the information which has been given and see what alternatives you would consider if it were your responsibility. It might remind you of other situations to which similar techniques might be applied, but in any case, it should give you food for thought.

No attempt has been made to cover the whole field of work study in this chapter. A number of techniques have been excluded and references to some aspects have been very brief. There are plenty of sources available where you can get more information and all I would like to add is that there is a lot of truth in the saying "Work study is only common sense".

Surely we can all apply that!

CHAPTER 13

New Manning Systems

IN HIS excellent book on *Ship Management*[4], Elden shows that, if fuel and port charges are excluded, owners spend twice as much on maintaining their ships as on operating them. He suggests, therefore, that shipowners should spend twice as much time and effort on reducing the maintenance costs as on reducing the operating costs. However, a close examination of current trends shows that this may not be happening and that owners both in Britain and abroad are concentrating more on reducing their crew numbers than on getting reliable machinery for their ships. The reduction in manning is usually associated with the introduction of sophisticated control devices in the engine-room but the point which is often overlooked is that these control devices are being fitted to (almost) traditional main engines and auxiliaries. These engines still require the same maintenance and yet, once control devices are fitted, there are usually less men to maintain these engines. Instead of decreasing, the personal work load on each engineer appears to be increasing in modern ships. Is this quite fair on our marine engineers?

There are a number of reasons for shipowners wanting to reduce the number of men needed to man their ships. One reason is to effect a saving in wages: an officer costs between £3000 and £4000 per year while a rating costs between £2000 and £3000 per year and, therefore, a reduction of only one man in the crew represents a real saving to the shipowner. Another reason is because of the world-wide shortage of engineers: so long as engineers remain in short supply, shipowners will be forced to fit such devices as will enable ships to run safely with less human supervision in the machinery spaces than there is at present. Still another reason is to reduce the weight and capital costs of ships. If we divide the weight and cost of the accommodation by the number of men carried we find that the accommodation for one man weighs about 15 tons and costs over £1000. Reducing the crew by one man certainly would not lighten the ship by 15 tons nor would she become £1000 cheaper to build but, if there were a considerable reduction in the crew, such ships would certainly be lighter and cheaper than when manned under traditional systems. The final reason for reducing crew numbers is not always appreciated by seamen: it is that both shipowners and unions are keen to upgrade the craftsmanship of seafarers and, by reducing the number of men on board and organizing them in a different way, those remaining on board will be forced to do different and more interesting work (usually with a higher technical content) than the work they do under traditional manning systems. To fit men for these new skills, training costs are bound to rise, but all sides agree that these training investments will be worth while if ships are made more efficient and crew members are given more satisfying tasks.

Many companies, both in Britain and abroad, are experimenting with dual- and general-purpose manning systems. By definition, dual-purpose manning means that the traditional deck and engine-room labour groups become interchangeable with the result that these men can be employed in both areas. General-purpose manning is a further development. In this system, all ratings form one work team and, while it is not common for (traditional) sailors and firemen to be used in catering duties, the stewards can be employed on deck during berthing and unberthing operations.

The size of this book precludes a description of the details concerning the manning of ships under these new systems and a few general remarks will have to suffice. The original experiments in dual- or general-purpose manning were carried out in tankers and bulk carriers which, of course, have no derricks, winches and cargo-lifting gear. Apart from the cleaning out of tanks and holds, and apart from the usual navigational watch-keeping duties, the work done by the deck crew in these ships consisted mainly of cleaning and painting. In loaded tankers with low freeboard, even these painting and cleaning duties were often prevented by seas and spray coming aboard. The result was that, in bad weather, the deck crew spent hours yarning under the focs'le head. Shore management observing this work pattern quite rightly asked if these men could not be employed in the engine room when bad weather and other causes (including lack of essential work) prevented them from working on deck.

Full discussions were held between management and unions and resulted in various experiments being carried out on dual-purpose manning. This new system has passed the experimental stage in tankers and bulk carrries and is now the accepted way of manning these ships.

Very few experiments have been carried out with dual-purpose manning of cargo ships (fitted with traditional cargo-handling gear) for the work pattern in these ships is quite different to that in ships which have no cargo gear. In traditional cargo ships, all the cargo gear has to be opened up, inspected and overhauled between ports. This can be an indoor job so, even when bad weather prevents outdoor work on deck, the deck crew can still be fully employed in maintaining the cargo gear. There is not the same need to find work for these men to do as there is in tankers under certain weather and loaded conditions. However, experiments are taking place and we look forward to getting the results.

The organizational and management philosophy adopted by most ships which carry dual- or general-purpose crews is to divide the roles and functions of the personnel aboard under the headings of "Operations" and "Maintenance". Instead of the work being planned by the head of each department, all planning is done by a management team consisting of the Master, Chief Engineer, Chief Officer, Second Engineer and, sometimes, the Chief Steward.

This management team meets at regular intervals, either once or twice a week and, after giving full consideration to the commitments of the ship and the maintenance work which needs to be done, decides on the order in which the work is to be carried out and on who is to do it. The concept of a management team is sound and should be encouraged in all ships even if they are manned under traditional systems.

One of the problems which has to be solved when considering the introduction of a new manning system is defining the exact duties and responsibilities of each man on board (particularly of the senior men) and to whom each is responsible. As the Master is responsible for the safety of life and the safety of the ship and, as he may hold ultimate responsibility in law for the sea-worthiness and cargo-worthiness of the ship and is responsible to the ship-owner for all factors affecting possible "Limitation of Liability" actions, it seems eminently sound to make everyone on board responsible to him as, in fact, has been the case for many years. However, one company has made the Master and Chief Engineer responsible directly to a shore manager—the Master for the general operation of the ship and the Chief Engineer for the mechanical reliability of the ship. This, of course, causes a division of responsibility on board and militates against the "management team" concept. An even worse suggested method is that the Master should be responsible to the Marine Superintendent for certain operational matters while the Chief Engineer should be responsible to the Technical Manager for all mechanical maintenance and engine operational matters. This idea not only militates against the team concept on board ship, but, in effect, creates a gulf or division throughout the company. It seems to me that the team concept must be fostered in both the ships and in the office ashore—to secure a sound communication system, if for no other reason. The different methods are illustrated in the following diagrams (Figs. 13.1, 13.2, 13.3). From these it can be seen that, if the flows of information coincide with the pattern of responsibility, the best system is to have management teams in both the ship and in the shore office.

Another problem which has arisen in introducing the new manning systems concerns the control of the ratings on board.

Should the dual-purpose team be under the Chief Officer or under the Chief Engineer? Most companies which have adopted these new manning systems have put the ratings under the Chief Engineer. Their argument has been that a ship is, essentially, a machine which floats and that practically all manual work can be classed as mechanical maintenance of one sort or another. It follows, therefore, that the man in charge of the mechanical

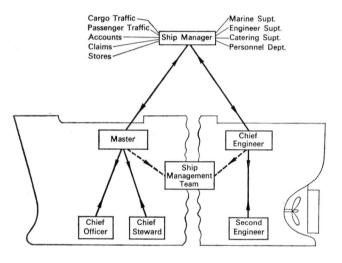

FIG. 13.1. Lines of communication when the Master and Chief Engineer are individually responsible to a ship manager ashore. A gulf exists between the personnel on board the ship.

maintenance should have full control of the working crew. Some companies, however, have left control of the ratings in the hands of the Chief Officer on the grounds that safety of ship and operational cargo efficiency must come first, and only if men can be spared from tasks concerning these two factors may they be released to the Chief Engineer for mechanical maintenance duties. It is also suggested by these latter companies that, traditionally, the Chief Officer (and the rest of the deck officers, for that matter) has always been the man to whom the crew have turned for directions and instructions on matters affecting their well-being and life on board ship; and there is a lot of evidence to support this contention. It is felt, by these companies, that the ratings would prefer to be under the Chief Officer. There is a lot of argument for and against both sides but, before we can come to some sort of conclusion, we should first get our priorities right. We must get things right not for the good of one department or the other but for the good of the Merchant Navy as a whole.

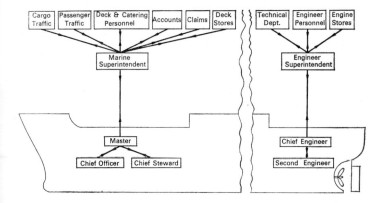

FIG. 13.2. Lines of communication when the Master is responsible to the Marine Superintendent and the Chief Engineer is responsible to the Engineer Superintendent. A gulf exists between personnel throughout the company.

Most people will agree that the whole purpose of a ship is to carry cargo or passengers quickly and safely from one port to another. This should be our first priority. Some people may argue that safety of life is, or should be, our first priority. Accidents, however, are contingencies and may, therefore, never happen. So let us redefine our first priority as being "the rapid and safe carriage of cargo from one port to another while being ready at all times to deal with any accidents, emergencies or dangers which may arise".

P.M.M.S.—G

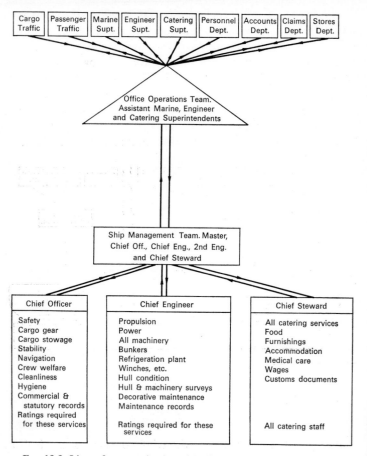

FIG. 13.3. Lines of communication when the management team on board is responsible to the management team ashore. Provided all communications move along the lines shown, everyone knows exactly what is going on.

Our second priority must surely be increasing the profit of our ships by reducing claims for damaged cargo and for personal injury to dockers and others, and by reducing the maintenance costs. Elden defines repair as taking care of something too late.

Thus we must have, as our second priority, the full and complete maintenance or care of the ship. Some of this maintenance will affect the sea-worthiness or cargo-worthiness of the ship, and this must come first. Other maintenance work will affect the efficient or speedy operation of the ship (in both cargo-handling and propulsion senses) and this must come next. The third class of maintenance work will concern the maintenance of the fabric and engines in order to reduce replacements required by the classification societies, and this must follow the previous classes of maintenance.

The third priority must be related to cleanliness. Lack of cleanliness may affect the safety of the ship (e.g. an accumulation of oil and rubbish presents a fire risk; spilled oil on a deck may present a potential hazard to anyone who walks across the area) and also the health and hygiene of the crew.

Finally there is decorative maintenance which makes the ship smarter to look at or more comfortable to live in. We could put this as fourth in our order of priorities.

If the various considerations listed above have been put in the correct order of priority then we can start to see a logical order of control emerging. As individuals, the various members of the management team will each have his own order of priorities but it is essential that the team as a whole and certainly the Master or man in charge, has the correct order of priorities as suggested above.

If the safe and speedy carriage of cargo and passengers is the first or most important priority, the man in charge—the Master —should have this as his personal first priority. Will a Chief Engineer who has devoted years to mechanical reliability and who derives a great deal of satisfaction and pride out of "keeping the job running" be able to switch his personal priorities? There are sure to be some men who will be able to accept the new first priority but why ask or expect men to change? The deck officers already have the speedy and safe carriage of cargo as their first priority. Should they not be left as the men in charge of the ship and should not they have first call on the dual-purpose labour group to achieve the safe and speedy carriage of cargo? The cargo work in which the crew are involved consists of cleaning and preparing holds for the reception of cargo, securing cargo, and overhauling cargo gear. Apart from the occasional cleaning of holds after very dirty cargoes, the crew's cargo work usually occupies a smaller part of their time than does their general maintenance work about the ship, particularly in ships which have long ocean passages between ports. Much of their day-to-day work at sea and in port is of a mechanical maintenance nature. Should not, therefore, the Chief Engineer be given the control of the dual-purpose labour squad?

There are some ships in which a considerable proportion of the crew's time is occupied with cargo matters, e.g. refrigerated ships in the meat trade and grain-carrying ships in which shifting boards have to be erected. If, in a particular ship, the deck crew are already fully employed on cargo work, then it would be undesirable to transfer these men to mechanical maintenance work under the Chief Engineer. Only a thorough job analysis will show whether a particular ship is suitable for being manned by a dual-purpose crew under the Chief Engineer and such an analysis should be carried out before any new manning methods are introduced. It is no use a manager saying that because dual-purpose manning works well in one type of ship it will, therefore, work in all types of ship.

On balance, then, it seems that if the ship is suitable, working control of the dual-purpose labour group should pass to the Chief Engineer. The Chief Officer should be in charge of all general employment, human and welfare matters affecting the crew and should have first call on these men for the efficient and safe working of the ship in an operational sense. The ultimate control will, of course, lie in the Master but he will exercise his authority through the management team. This system is illustrated in Fig. 13.3.

In order to give all members of the dual-purpose labour group an equal share of the various types of work aboard ship, it will be necessary to rotate men between the different jobs, each spending a month or a passage on each type of job.

Another problem which has arisen as a result of the new

manning systems is that of job satisfaction for the Chief Officer. Under traditional manning systems, Chief Officers are one of the busiest—if not *the* busiest—men on board. Not only does he have a watch to keep but at sea he has to devote a great deal of time and effort to the maintenance of the ship and in port to the stowage, separation and securing of cargo.

In tankers and bulk carriers, much of the Chief Officer's role as a cargo officer has been taken from him—these bulk cargoes are usually loaded and discharged by shore appliances and there are very few problems of stowage, separation, contamination and securing with these cargoes. The growing use of containers will cause a similar reduction in the Chief Officer's cargo role aboard general cargo ships. Now, with the introduction of the dual-purpose manning systems, even the maintenance role is being taken away from the Chief Officer leaving him, apparently, with very little to do except keep a watch. The deck officer group as a whole fears and resents this gradual whittling away of their spheres of work and responsibility. Some members of this group suggest that the only reason for introducing these new manning systems was to find a job for the Chief Engineer!

On close examination, however, it can be seen that at long last the deck officers are freed of their day-to-day maintenance worries in order to become true "Operational Officers". This is their correct role, but they will need to be properly trained if they are to carry out this (almost) new role effectively—particularly if it involves the monitoring of any machinery or instruments. The mechanical, electrical and electronic engineering knowledge of the average deck officer at sea today is abysmally poor and the greatest and most urgent need of deck officers is to have their engineering knowledge upgraded. They need not know how to repair or maintain sophisticated machinery or equipment but they certainly need to understand all the operational features of the machinery aboard if they are to monitor the machinery in ships with unmanned engine rooms and if they are to operate their ships at maximum efficiency. A very strong case can be made for compelling all operations officers of the future to attend courses of three or four years' duration instead of the three- or four-month courses which are being talked about at present.

Even without lengthy training, deck officers could, by the use of one or two new instruments, operate their ships more efficiently than they do at present. By tradition, a ship embarking on a long ocean passage follows a great circle course no matter what the weather may be on that route. The only reason for following this course is that it is the shortest distance between two points on the earth's surface. What is sometimes overlooked is that a route which is shortest in distance may not be the one which is shortest in time yet it is an early and safe arrival which should be our first consideration when choosing a particular course. It is common in many ships to lay off courses before departure from a port and then to stick to those courses (steaming at whatever speed the Chief Engineer can give) no matter what the weather may turn out to be. Most Masters will defend this system of navigation on the grounds that they lack up to date information on the weather in their areas. At last, however, an instrument is available which produces up to date weather information for no more effort than the turning of a switch. The instrument is the Facsimile Weather Recorder which actually draws synoptic and forecast weather charts and wave patterns for many parts of the world. By using the latest weather information, the Master and Navigating Officers of a ship can choose the fastest passage across an ocean even if this route calls for frequent alterations of course. Ships already fitted with these recorders have found that they can, for example, save between six and thirty hours on a passage from the Caribbean to Europe, while the officers on these ships find that their time is well occupied in evaluating the weather information received. Weather routing is the coming thing in shipping and it is probable that, in time, we will look on the Facsimile Weather Recorder as the most important instrument fitted in ships since the introduction of radar.

The dual-purpose manning system, described earlier in this chapter, is one change that is taking place in the traditional manning of ships, but it is not the only one.

The fitting of self-tensioning winches, automatic pilots and call systems, means for using pre-prepared food by micro wave cookers, etc., allow a shipowner to reduce the number of the crew without, necessarily, having to adopt the dual-purpose system. In fact it may be found that, because of the different work patterns in the two types of ships, dual-purpose manning systems will be used in bulk carriers while traditional manning systems will continue to be used in ordinary dry cargo ships. As was mentioned earlier, it is wholly wrong to say that because one system is good for one type of ship it is, therefore, good for all types of ships.

Still another development in manning which is starting to gain ground came from a suggestion put forward in shipping newspapers in 1967[9, 12, 22]. The scope of this book prevents me from going into the economic details but a case can be made for a shipowner building a hull to suit his particular trade and then hiring or leasing all his main propulsion and auxiliary machinery from an engine builder under a contract in which the engine builder undertakes to design, install, man and maintain the machinery in the ship. This will mean that the engineers will be the employees of the engine builder. Many problems and difficulties will spring to mind but all can be overcome by correct planning and by the correct wording of contracts. The main point is that, as they will be the employees of an engine builder, marine engineers will be able to alternate periods at sea with periods ashore at the builder's works. Not only will a man employed in this way enjoy a better family life than marine engineers do at present but he will also be able to see a clear career path ahead of him in marine engineering.

Many suggestions have been put forward on attracting and keeping the right number of engineers at sea. These suggestions have ranged from short service commissions and gratuities to offering engineers command of a ship. The former suggestion has some merit and could possibly be applied to all merchant seamen. The second suggestion is, in my opinion, not at all sound and is usually defended on the grounds that engineers leave the sea

because they "cannot get to the top". This is not true, for an
engineer can be promoted to Engineer Superintendent and, what
is more important, he can, because of his training and experience
in charge of large power plants, usually rise faster in certain
industries ashore than can any ex-deck officer with his more
specialized training and experience. As I have already mentioned,
the whole world is suffering from a chronic shortage of trained
engineers and engineering training facilities, and it seems to me
quite wrong to suggest peeling a trained engineer away from his
career in marine engineering and retraining him for command of
ships. I think it is worth mentioning that this suggestion of
engineers rising to command rarely comes from the men actually
at sea; it usually comes from technical men ashore. I would
suggest that the best way of attracting engineers to the shipping
industry is by offering them a clear career path in engineering,
and one way of doing this is by making them the employees of
the engine builders so that ultimate shore employment may be
guaranteed to them. Evidence to support this suggestion may be
found from examining the employment of radio officers at
sea.

Some shipping companies employ their own radio officers and
men entering the direct employ of a shipping company know that
they are being recruited for a life-time at sea. Most shipping
companies, however, hire their radio equipment and radio
officers from one of the large radio companies. The largest of
these radio companies guarantees ultimate shore employment to
all its radio officers and, as a result, has little difficulty in recruiting the required number of men. On the other hand, those
shipping companies who try to recruit their own radio officers,
find the greatest difficulty in attracting the number of men
they require and, consequently, many of their ships are manned
by radio officers seconded from one of the large radio companies.
Does this not support the view that one of the most effective ways
of recruiting men to the Merchant Navy is to guarantee them
ultimate shore employment? If men can feel sure that they will
eventually be offered shore employment will they not be more

likely to stay at sea longer than those men who, not having this guarantee, feel that they should start looking for shore employment before it is too late?

There are still further effects of the new manning systems. Traditionally deck officers have directed labour rather than engaged in physical work themselves. This may change and they may be expected to carry out more physical work. Also, there has always been a gulf between officers and ratings and, with three ratings in a watch under traditional schemes, this may not have been a matter of concern for some officers. Now that we have many ships with only one rating in a watch, and this kept on the bridge, the gap between officers and ratings should be narrowing. Officers must accept the new developments and, wherever possible, should encourage their one rating to become involved in the navigating of the ship.

Suggestions are already being made that there should be a new certificate—a Watchkeeper's certificate. Ratings with the necessary sea time have always been allowed to sit for their Second Mate's certificates, but the conditions under which they have to study and the mathematical content of this certificate mean that most ratings have difficulty in obtaining their Second Mate's certificate. However, if this simpler Watchkeeper's certificate were introduced, it should be within the reach of many ratings.

There are many different ways of manning a ship but, before any one system is adopted, the shipowner must decide on his maintenance philosophy. He must decide whether all but the biggest jobs are to be carried out by the ship's crew or whether most of the maintenance work is to be done by shore labour with the ship's crew only employed in light preventative maintenance and carrying out emergency repairs. It is only when this decision is taken that thought can be given to the minimum number of men required to man a particular ship. I also believe that it will be quite wrong to draw up minimum manning scales for ships of various sizes; the peculiarities and trade of each ship must be taken into account.

Any new manning structure introduced into a modern ship should, so far as possible, meet the following conditions:

1. The number of men carried should be the minimum required for the safety, operational *and* maintenance needs of that ship, taking into account any unusual features of the ship and the trade in which she is engaged.

2. The manning structure should not temporarily create new roles which will be superseded by machines and/or computers in the next generation of ships, some ten years hence. Nor must the manning scheme call for types of men who are just not obtainable at present.

3. The organization and control on board should coincide with the departmental organization in the company's office ashore, i.e. it is no use having the Chief Engineer on board responsible to the Master and then, in the office ashore, having the (Deck) Marine Superintendent answerable to the Technical Manager of Engineer Superintendent; conflicts already apparent in some companies will be exacerbated.

CHAPTER 14

Seafarers' Organizations

WHEN we look at the Merchant Navy we find, at the core, a large body of men who go to sea. Surrounding this core are a number of organizations, the aim of each being to control, protect, or secure the welfare of seamen. Some of these organizations are hundreds of years old while others only came into existence during this present century. There are so many of these organizations that it would be impossible to describe each one in detail here and, therefore, only a few of the more important organizations will be described.

The Board of Trade

From a legal point of view, the most important organization affecting seafarers is the Shipping Department of the Board of Trade. This department is divided into three sections: the Marine Section; the Shipping Operations, Ports and Planning Section; and the Shipping Policy Section. Of these three sections the one most closely related to the subject of this book is the Marine Section; it is this section which applies the law contained in the Merchant Shipping Acts. The work of this section covers safety of ships, passengers and seamen; sea-worthiness of hulls, equipment and machinery; construction rules; load-lines; life saving appliances; lights and sound signals; radio; pilotage; salvage; wreck; lighthouses and marks; tonnage; and a number of other regulations affecting safety at sea. The Marine Section is, in turn, divided into three divisions: the Marine Safety Division; the Marine Crews Division; and the Marine Navigational Aids Division. Only the first two divisions will be dealt with in this chapter.

The Marine Survey Service applies the law relating to safety at sea and has three branches. These branches are headed by the Chief Nautical Surveyor, the Engineer Surveyor-in-Chief, and the Chief Ship Surveyor. These Chief Surveyors head teams of surveyors who are qualified in one of the branches mentioned above. A Nautical Surveyor must hold an Extra Master's certificate and must have been in command of foreign-going ships; an Engineer Surveyor should hold an Extra First Class certificate and must have been at sea; and a Ship Surveyor must be a naval architect with experience in the design and construction of ships. These Surveyors may be stationed at the headquarters in London or in one of the nine districts into which the United Kingdom has been divided for survey purposes.

Nautical Surveyors carry out inspections of ship's life saving and fire-fighting appliances; they check on the manning of ships; and they examine deck officers for their certificates of competency and ratings for Efficient Deck Hand certificates and lifeboatmen certificates. Engineer Surveyors carry out inspections of ships' hulls and machinery and examine engineer officers for their certificates of competency. Ship Surveyors may carry out surveys and check on all the calculations related to the load-lines, tonnage and stability of ships. All these surveyors have the power to detain any ship, British or foreign, which they consider to be unseaworthy.

The Marine Crews Division applies the law relating to the employment of men at sea. The headquarters are at London and Cardiff and, in all major ports, the work of this division is carried out by the Superintendents of Mercantile Marine Offices. The officers in this Marine Crews Division witness the engagement and discharge of crews; check on accommodation, food and medical supplies; and deal with the repatriation of distressed British seamen. In ports out of the United Kingdom, the work of this division is done by H.M. Consular Officers or by the appropriate Commonwealth Officers.

The General Register and Record of Shipping and Seamen is at Cardiff, and here all records are kept. Copies are kept of

Articles of Agreement, ships' official logbooks and the personal records of all seamen—their qualifications, ships in which they have served, and reports they have received from Masters.

The National Maritime Board

The next most important organization affecting seamen is the National Maritime Board which came into existence on a permanent basis in 1920.

The purposes of the N.M.B. are:

(1) to prevent and adjust any differences between shipowners, Masters, seamen and apprentices;

(2) to establish, revise and maintain a national standard rate (or rates) of wages and conditions of employment throughout the Merchant Navy; and

(3) to establish a single source of supply of seamen jointly controlled by shipowners and unions so arranged that a shipowner will have the right to select his own crew; a seaman will have the right to select his ship and equal rights of registration and employment will be secured for all seamen.

The National Maritime Board is formed of six panels. On each panel there are twelve representatives from each side. There are two chairmen of the N.M.B., one elected by either side, and one of whom takes the chair at alternate meetings. The same system of two chairmen, each taking the chair at alternate meetings, applies to each panel as it does to the whole National Maritime Board. No chairman has a casting vote; no resolution may be carried unless it has been approved by the majority of members present at a meeting.

The six panels which together form the National Maritime Board are:

(1) The Shipmasters' Panel.
(2) The Navigating Officers' Panel.
(3) The Engineer Officers' Panel.

    (4)   The Radio Officers' Panel.

    (5)   The Sailors' and Firemen's Panel.

    (6)   The Catering Department Panel.

The owners' representatives on each panel are elected by the British Shipping Federation. The employees' representatives are elected by the Mercantile Marine Service Association and the Merchant Navy and Airline Officers' Association (M.N.A.O.A.) on the Shipmasters' Panel; by the M.N.A.O.A. on the Navigating and Engineer Officers' Panels; by the Radio Officers' Union on the Radio Officers' Panel; and by the National Union of Seamen on the Sailors' and Firemen's and on the Catering Department Panels. One seat on the employers' side is allocated to the British Railways Board and one to the Naval Director of Stores. On the employees' side of the Sailors' and Firemen's Panel, one seat is allocated to the Shipconstructors' and Shipwrights' Association, now amalgamated with the Boilermakers' Society, which represents sea-going carpenters.

In addition to the main panels of the N.M.B., district panels are established at most major ports. These district panels appoint Port Consultants whose duty it is to secure the prompt manning of vessels and to avoid delays by settling any problems which may arise in connection with the engagement and discharge of seamen. These Port Consultants have no power to alter any agreements made by the National Maritime Board.

The National Maritime Board publishes a Year Book[14] which contains full details of all the wages and conditions of employment which have been agreed upon by the National Maritime Board. These conditions are binding on all seamen for, in each set of ships' Articles, a clause is inserted which binds everyone on board to N.M.B. conditions and to any changes in these conditions which may be made during the currency of the Articles.

The National Maritime Board is widely held, throughout the world, to be an ideal form of industrial negotiating machinery. On the other hand, it was criticized in the Pearson Report[20] as causing over-centralization in the Merchant Navy and as preventing shipowners from negotiating wages and conditions best suited to their particular ships or trades. Many shipowners defend the system of a national wage and employment structure on the grounds that it prevents the "leap-frogging" of wages.

The Established Service Scheme

This scheme was introduced in 1947 to replace the Reserve Pool (which had been established by an Essential Work Order during the war) and to combat the casual nature of seagoing employment which had been the case before the war.

The whole purpose of this scheme is to provide some security of employment and to provide a single source of supply of seamen. This source is jointly controlled by the employers (the British Shipping Federation) and by the employees (the Officers' Associations and the National Union of Seamen). Under this scheme, neither the Federation nor the National Union of Seamen can insist on the employment of any rating who is unacceptable to the other.

The British Shipping Federation is responsible for administering the scheme and meets the costs involved. Two forms of contract are offered—the general service contract, under which a man may be sent to a ship of any company, and the company service contract, under which a man is employed on the ships of one company only. Provided a seaman has a certificate of competency or has completed the necessary seatime, he may be offered a contract. Whether a seaman accepts the contract or not is left entirely to the man himself; he is not forced to accept a contract under the Established Service Scheme.

The number of U.K. domiciled seafarers actually serving at present is about 40,000 officers and 60,000 ratings. (This excludes 31,000 non-European ratings, mainly Indians, who enter into engagements in their country of origin). The U.K. seafarers may serve under a company service contract, or under a general service contract, or be unestablished.

At present about 17,000 officers and about 8500 ratings are

serving under company contracts and are the responsibility of the individual companies. About 1500 officers and 20,000 ratings have general service contracts, by which they undertake to serve on any ship as directed by the Merchant Navy Establishment, which on its side, undertakes either to find them employment or to pay "establishment benefit". In recent years, although the total number of seafarers has been falling, the proportion serving under one or other form of contract has been increasing. The terms of these contracts are now being reviewed and the proportion should further increase as a result.

The Merchant Navy Establishment also matches vacancies with the remaining officers and ratings who are "unestablished", either because they are not yet eligible for a contract or prefer not to enter into one. The total number of seafarers, unestablished or under general service contract, supplied to companies by the Merchant Navy Establishment in the twelve months up to 2 December 1967 was approximately 164,000.

An "established" seaman receives a number of benefits from the scheme, apart from the guarantee of employment for two years at a time. If no employment is available for him between ships, he will receive establishment benefit which is a weekly payment based on his last earnings and which is paid over and above National Insurance unemployment benefits. He may also be paid extra sickness benefits on the same scale as establishment benefits. An established seaman will also be paid while studying for certificates of competency or while attending other approved courses.

A seaman will only be offered a contract if he is of proved character and ability and if he is physically fit for service; his contract will only be renewed if his record of conduct and ability remains satisfactory. If any seaman fails to carry out his obligations under the Establishment Scheme, or if he is guilty of inefficiency or misconduct prejudicial to discipline, then he may be "Cautioned", "Suspended" or have his contract "Terminated" by the administration.

The British Shipping Federation Limited

The British Shipping Federation is the national representative organization of United Kingdom merchant shipowners (but not the fishing fleet) for all matters relating to seagoing personnel. Other matters of common concern to shipowners, broadly described as economic and commercial, are handled by the Chamber of Shipping of the United Kingdom.

The present title dates from 1st January 1967, when the existing Shipping Federation amalgamated with the Seafarers' Committee of the Employers Association of the Port of Liverpool, although the two bodies had worked closely together for many years. The original Shipping Federation was founded in September 1890 as an employers' association to match the seafarers' unions then coming into being. The age in which it was founded was one of hostility between employer and workman. They were the days when stubborn resistance was countered by ugly violence; when Federation "ticket" crews were smuggled on board at dead of night to avoid pickets and when Federation officials were often stoned on sight. The situation has now been completely transformed and, today, we find spokesmen of shipowners and seafarers meeting quietly together to reach business-like agreements. The credit for the transformation belongs to those far-sighted leaders on both sides who came to realise that their interests were joint, not separate, and to the growth of that humane spirit which has moulded industrial relations into their modern shape. The reader, wishing to trace the development of the Shipping Federation from those early, turbulent years to the present, should refer to the excellent book *The Shipping Federation* by L. H. Powell, published on the occasion of the Federation's Diamond Jubilee.

The functions of the Federation have been greatly extended since its incorporation and are described below under the following headings:

(a) General policy.
(b) Negotiations on pay and conditions of work.

(c) Recruitment.
(d) Placement.
(e) Training.
(f) Welfare.
(g) Miscellaneous.

In the discharge of these functions the British Shipping Federation acts, in some cases, as a policy-making and in others as an executive body, and in some cases as both. In some cases it provides the administrative machinery for formulating and carrying out the policies of separate organizations on which it is represented.

Virtually the whole of the British shipping industry, consisting of about 400 companies, is represented in the British Shipping Federation either directly or through the Protecting and Indemnity Associations. The British Shipping Federation, together with the Merchant Navy Establishment (Section D), has a total staff of about 500, of whom about 100 are in its London headquarters and the remainder in its 17 districts. (The district organization is at present under review, and the number of districts is likely to be considerably reduced.)

A. General policy

The British Shipping Federation negotiates with the appropriate government departments on legislation or regulations affecting personnel. Examples are the current revision of the Merchant Shipping Act, 1894, resulting from Lord Pearson's Committee of Inquiry; Selective Employment Tax; the Redundancy Payments Act, 1965; and the Board of Trade's manning regulations. Evidence has recently been submitted to Lord Donovan's Royal Commission on Trade Unions and Employers' Associations and to Lord Rochdale's Committee of Inquiry on British Shipping. The Federation plays a part in national industrial policy through its representation on the Confederation of British Industry's Labour and Social Affairs Committee.

It is represented on the International Shipping Federation

(and provides its secretariat) and on the International Labour Organization's Joint Maritime Commission.

B. *Negotiations on pay and conditions of work*

As is mentioned elsewhere in this chapter, rates of pay and conditions of work for U.K. domiciled seafarers are the subject of National Maritime Board agreements. The British Shipping Federation nominates the employers' representatives to each panel on the N.M.B. and to the District Maritime Boards.

The Federation has its own internal committees and sub-committees to give guidance to its N.M.B. representatives. An important example is the Productivity Committee, which is at present mainly concerned with arrangements for "general purpose" crewing.

C. *Recruitment*

This subject is closely linked with the two following sections. Officers are recruited both by individual companies and by the British Shipping Federation, and ratings by the Federation only. The Federation issues literature, conducts press advertising and poster campaigns, and has seven Selection Officers in the major ports who attend careers conventions, give talks to schools and other organizations and advise prospective entrants.

D. *Placement*

The British Shipping Federation runs the Merchant Navy Establishment, which operates as a labour exchange through 30 offices and three agencies in 29 ports. The Establishment Scheme is described elsewhere in this chapter.

E. *Training*

The British Shipping Federation is concerned with training both as a policy matter and executively.

Course	Location	Duration	Numbers trained during the 12 months ended 30th Sept. 1967
Engineer Officers Group Courses for Junior Engineers	Southampton College of Technology	3 months	87
Marine Engineer Officer Scholarship Course	South Shields Marine & Technical College	14 weeks	19
E.R. Certificate Course	Leith Nautical College	2 years	5
Operators' Course	Leith Nautical College	1 year	7
Engineer Cadet Training Scheme	Various Colleges approved by B.O.T.	2 years	490 (O.N.D.)* 188 (O.N.C.)* 90 (Pt. "A")*
A.B.'s Certificate	National Sea Training Schools (7 schools)	1 week	171
E.D.H.'s Certificate	National Sea Training Schools (7 schools)	1 week	1293
D.H.U.'s Certificate	National Sea Training Schools (3 schools)	2 weeks	97
Lifeboat Certificate	National Sea Training Schools (7 schools)	1 week	1854
Chief & Prospective Chief Stewards	Liverpool Nautical Catering College	3 weeks	74
Assistant Stewards Adult Catering Refresher	National Sea Training School, London Liverpool Nautical Catering College	1 week 2 weeks	283 83
Adult Catering New Entrants	Highbury Technical College, Portsmouth	3 weeks	133
Ship's Cook Certificate	National Sea Training Schools (3 schools) Other Colleges	6 weeks 6 weeks	109 232

Course	Location	Duration	Numbers trained during the 12 months ended 30th Sept. 1967
Ship's Cook's Higher Certificate	National Sea Training Schools (3 schools) Other Colleges	3 weeks 3 weeks	22 19
Ships' Cook Higher Certificate Refresher	National Sea Training Schools (3 schools) Other Colleges	1 week 1 week	11 11
Engine room Ratings	National Sea Training Schools (1 school)	3 weeks	462
Deck Ratings Boy Entry	National Sea Training Schools (3 schools) Other Schools	12 weeks Various	991 242
Catering Ratings Boy Entry	National Sea Training Schools (1 school) Other schools	8 weeks Various	1422 143
Personnel Relations	British Shipping Federation courses at various centres	3 days	392
Fire Fighting Officers Ratings	Fire Stations at major seaports	1–3 days	858 1830
Work Study Appreciation	Slough College	4 days	130
Tanker Safety Course	School of Navigation, Southampton	5 days	613
Supervisors' Courses for Petty Officers	Various Centres	5 days	20†

*Estimated numbers   †Pilot Course

Note: This statement does not refer to O.N.D. courses in Nautical Science and degree courses for navigation officers, nor does it refer to pre-sea and mid-cadetship release course for navigating cadets as they are not co-ordinated or arranged by the British Shipping Federation.

(a) Policy is decided by the Merchant Navy Training Board, on which shipowners, government departments, educationalists, nautical colleges and the seafarers' organizations are represented. The Federation provides the secretariat, and its present chairman is also chairman of the Board. The M.N.T.B.'s work is described elsewhere in this chapter.

(b) (i) The Federation is the executive arm of the National Sea Training Trust, which is financed jointly by it and the Department of Education and Science, and at present the Director of the Federation is its chairman. The Trust administers the National Sea Training School and 12 schools for serving ratings throughout the country. The National Sea Training School, whose new buildings at Gravesend were completed at the end of 1966, has a staff of 75 and boarding accommodation for 570 boys: the great majority of intending deck and catering ratings receive their pre-sea training there.

(ii) The Merchant Navy cadet training school H.M.S. *Conway* is in process of being taken over jointly by Cheshire County Council and the British Shipping Federation, which will have a majority on the board of governors.

(iii) The British Shipping Federation is directly responsible for a large number of courses on different subjects for seafarers of various categories, in some cases co-ordinating the efforts of the nautical and technical colleges and in others running the courses itself.

The courses arranged or co-ordinated by the British Shipping Federation are shown on pages 204–5.

F. Welfare

The British Shipping Federation is represented on the Merchant Navy Welfare Board, together with 35 voluntary organizations, seafarers' organizations and government departments. The Board co-ordinates welfare arrangements and appeals for public money, and administers seven residential hotels and two non-residential clubs.

G. *Miscellaneous*

(a) PENSIONS. The Merchant Navy Officers' Pension Fund is a contributory scheme administered jointly by the Federation and the officers' organizations. The Merchant Navy Ratings' Pension Fund is a non-contributory scheme started in 1965, financed by shipowners and administered by Federation trustees.

(b) PERSONAL INJURIES. The Federation deals with claims against shipowners under the Workmen's Compensation Acts and at Common Law. It also records and analyses all accidents to seafarers and conducts a safety campaign by means of posters, booklets and courses.

(c) MEDICAL. The Federation has a staff of nearly 100 full-time and part-time doctors in the ports.

(d) WORK STUDY. A work study department has recently been set up in conjunction with the Chamber of Shipping.

It can be seen from the above that the Federation is taking constructive steps to produce smooth and efficient operation of our merchant ships and, in so doing, is playing a major role in securing the prosperity of the British Merchant Navy and of the country as a whole.

Many of the officials in the Federation are men with legal training and are able to advise shipowners on any legal matters affecting employment in the industry. The Federation, as has been mentioned above, also employs doctors to give advice on medical matters. But much of the work of the Federation concerns the recruitment, selection and training of men and it is hard to understand why the Federation does not employ trained educationalists and psychologists to give sound advice to the industry as a whole, or to individual shipping companies, on human and educational matters. The recent engagement of an experienced Work Study Officer was a step in the right direction for this man is now in a position to advise the shipping industry on all aspects of work study.

The National Union of Seamen

In 1887, the National Amalgamated Sailors' and Firemen's Union was founded and, in 1894 the name of this union was changed to the National Sailors' and Firemen's Union. In 1926 the name was again changed to the National Union of Seamen.

The objects of this Union are:

(1) To promote and to provide funds to extend the adoption of trade union principles;

(2) to improve the conditions and protect the interests of all members of the Union;

(3) to endeavour to obtain reasonable hours of duty and fair wages for members;

(4) to provide funds for the relief of the members during legitimate trade disputes connected with the seafaring industry;

(5) to assist and protect all officials, employees, and members of the Union whose interests have been damaged by reason of their services to the Union;

(6) to use every legitimate effort to provide for the safety of ships' work in order to prevent accidents and loss of life;

(7) to ensure the proper and adequate manning of all ships;

(8) to keep a careful watch on the scale of free-board on all vessels;

(9) to ensure the fixing of proper and adequate shifting boards in all vessels carrying homogenous cargoes;

(10) to ensure greater stability in the construction of ships;

(11) to ensure improved and adequate accommodation for seamen in all vessels and seamen's establishments ashore, to promote the general welfare of seafarers, and the maintenance of crew sanitary accommodation;

(12) to provide funds for the relief of financial members meeting with accidents in following their employment excepting all such accidents as may be directly attributable to the carelessness, insobriety, or culpable negligence of the members;

(13) to provide funds to assist in defraying the cost incurred in consequence of the death of any financial member of the Union, or his wife;

(14) to provide funds for the relief of financial members who may suffer loss of their personal effects by reason of shipwreck, fire or other disaster on board ship;

(15) to provide funds for the payment of contributions of members who are unable themselves to do so through sickness or unemployment;

(16) to provide legal assistance to financial members in respect of matters arising out of or incidental to their employment;

(17) to provide an efficient class of men for the Mercantile Marine;

(18) to provide funds for the provision of old age grants to financial members who are in compliance with the rules;

(19) to provide funds from members and others to assist in the maintenance and upkeep of rest homes, hospitals and the furtherance of other projects catering for the needs of seamen;

(20) to provide educational facilities for seamen;

(21) to regulate the relations between employer and employees;

(22) to provide funds for a superannuation scheme for all officials and employees;

(23) to secure provision for insurance by the owners to cover loss of or damage to the effects of the crew in any circumstances; and

(24) to provide funds for the political objects of the Union and the furtherance of political representation.

All seamen, of either sex, are eligible for membership of the Union. A "financial member" is one who has been a member for at least twelve months and who is not more than thirteen weeks in arrears of contribution.

The branches are the basic units of the Union's structure. It is here where motions are tabled and debated and from whence resolutions go to higher authorities of the Union. There are forty branches in the United Kingdom and Ireland and ten offices in other parts of the world. Each branch has its own full-time secretary and officials.

The forty branches are grouped into seven administrative districts each under the supervision of a district secretary who is the chief negotiating officer of the Union for the area he covers.

The supreme authority of the Union is the Annual General Meeting which is held in various places throughout Britain and Ireland. Each district elects its delegates and the total number in attendance at the A.G.M. is 141; forty-five are officials, thirty-three are the elected seagoing members of the Executive Council and sixty-three are ordinary members. Various resolutions are debated and the Annual General Meeting lays down the general policy the Union is to follow for the coming year.

In between the annual general meetings, the Union is run by the Executive Council which consists of thirty-three ordinary members, twelve officials and three trustees. The aim of this council is to see that the Union is run properly and that the policies laid down at the A.G.M. are pursued.

The Executive Council meets quarterly (or more often if required) and cannot make a detailed study of every subject in the time it has at its disposal. Thus a smaller group of fifteen executive councillors is formed known as the Finance and General Purposes Committee. It deals principally with money and property matters but it also has the power to make decisions on other urgent matters, but unless these decisions are ratified by the Executive Council, they cease to operate.

The day-to-day administration is in the hands of the General Secretary assisted by three Assistant General Secretaries, a National Organizer and a number of officials at head office. The General Secretary is elected by means of a postal ballot of all members.

Although there were a number of unofficial strikes during the mid 1920's and in the late 1950's, the last official strike called by this union (prior to the 1966 strike) was in 1912. This is surely evidence of the responsible attitude of the officials and members of this union and, if they keep up their record, the next official strike should not be before the year 2020! The National Union of Seamen has a very important role to play in securing the prosperity of the Merchant Navy and, indeed, of everyone in Britain. I feel sure that they will continue to display the same degree of responsibility in the future as they have done in the past.

The Officers' Associations

In 1857, the primary object of the founders of the Mercantile Marine Service Association was to establish an organization capable of taking all possible action to raise the status of the British Mercantile Marine officer and to promote the general interests of the service. These aims remain unchanged today but, in comparatively recent years, there has been something of a shift of emphasis in the M.M.S.A.'s own contribution to this work, its primary function now being to apply itself more particularly to the professional and industrial affairs of British shipmasters alone. The work towards the more general advancement of officers' interests as a whole is carried out by the Merchant Navy and Airline Officers' Association (founded in 1936) with which the M.M.S.A. works in the closest co-operation. Both these Associations are affiliated to the Officers' (Merchant Navy) Federation.

In all the developments which have led up to the present situation none is of greater significance than the progressive elimination of wasteful inter-organizational rivalry. To the credit of all concerned this has not been brought about by ruthless elimination. Rather has it come through the growing realization that all were working towards a common goal and that real advancement in the interests of shipmasters and officers could only be obtained by friendly co-operation and united effort. Logically this trend led to the amalgamation of the M.M.S.A. and the Imperial Merchant Service Guild in 1936; the affiliation of the M.M.S.A. to the Officers' (Merchant Navy) Federation in 1942;

and the merger of the Navigators' and Engineer Officers' Union with the Marine Engineers' Association in 1956.

The Merchant Navy and
Airline Officers' Association

The Merchant Navy and Airline Officers' Association is the largest Merchant Navy officers' association in the world. It looks after the interests of navigating, engineer, Purser and medical officers and navigating and engineer cadets in the ships of the British Merchant Navy, and of navigators and flight engineers in civil airlines.

In view of the special nature of service in the Merchant Navy and airlines, which is civilian employment yet very different from most other civilian occupations, the Association has to deal with a very extensive range of subjects affecting its members, and numerous personal problems of most various kinds, in addition to such everyday matters as improving and safeguarding pay, conditions of service, leave, and other matters of employment. It provides legal defence for those members who, unfortunately, may sometimes have to appear before a Court of Inquiry, and it provides compensation if the certificate of competency of a member is suspended or cancelled as a result of such an inquiry.

As the Merchant Navy and airlines have so many international aspects and contracts, perhaps more than any other industry, it is inevitable that the Association is concerned in many international activities, and takes part in the meetings and activities of many international, as well as national, bodies and committees. Through affiliation to the Officers' (Merchant Navy) Federation, the Association is linked with officers' organizations in several British Commonwealth countries.

The Merchant Navy and Airline Officers' Association was formed originally as the Navigators' and Engineer Officers' Union in 1936. It took its present title after a merger with the Marine Engineers' Association in April 1956. It is affiliated to the

Trades Union Congress and the International Transport Workers' Federation, but it is strictly a non-political organization.

The objects of the M.N.A.O.A. are:

(a) to regulate conditions of employment between members and their employers;

(b) to foster and develop the best interests of all undertakings in which members are employed and of all those engaged therein;

(c) to promote generally the welfare of members;

(d) to establish superannuation or benefit schemes, contributory or otherwise, in conjunction with the employers, or otherwise, for members;

(e) to secure proper and adequate manning of ships and aircraft;

(f) to take all necessary action in regard to national and international legislation, conventions, rules, recommendations and regulations and their furtherance and observance in the interests of the industries concerned and those engaged therein;

(g) to join or participate in the work or activities of such national and international bodies or conferences as the Council may determine for the purpose of influencing such legislation, conventions, rules, recommendations and regulations as such bodies or conferences may be considering;

(h) to provide benefits for members including sickness, unemployment, unemployment arising from trade disputes duly recognized by the Council, also in such other circumstances as the Council may from time to time determine;

(i) to make from time to time, but only during such times as the Council may determine, provision of benefits to members and/or their widows and other dependants where the Council considers necessary, subject to and conditional upon the right of the Council at any time to extend by schemes or otherwise suspend, vary or cancel any benefit at any time without notice;

(j) to promote and participate in the work of any body, national or international, charged with or considering the selection, control of entry and training of officers and apprentices for the sea and air services, and for the regulations of their conditions generally;

(k) to provide such legal advice and service for members as may be considered necessary or desirable;

(l) to make grants and endowments to hospitals, sanatoriums, convalescent homes, institutions, training schemes, charities and recognized welfare schemes for the benefit of members and their dependants;

(m) to participate financially or otherwise, directly or indirectly, in the establishment or carrying on of the business of printing or publishing of a journal or newspaper, books, literature or publications;

(n) to participate financially or otherwise, directly or indirectly, in the establishment or carrying on of any company business or project whether commercial or otherwise which is considered by the Council to further the interests of members;

(o) to further any other action or purpose by the participation financially or otherwise, directly or indirectly, including the acquisition of any class of shares, in any undertaking, commercial or otherwise, which in the opinion of the Council further the interests of the members;

(p) for all or any of the above objects the Association by its Council shall have power, *inter alia*:

    (i) to utilize subscriptions, entrance fees, income from all sources, and moneys invested by the Association;

    (ii) to own, purchase, lease, mortage, or otherwise deal with lands or property;

    (iii) to erect and furnish such buildings as may be considered necessary or desirable;

    (iv) to establish superannuation or benefit schemes, contributory or otherwise, for officials and employees of the Association;

(v) to invest, in the names of the trustees, all Association moneys and funds in such securities, shares, debentures, mortgages and loans including commercial and industrial undertakings as the Council may determine;

(q) for the purpose of fulfilling any object there may be established, out of the Association's funds or assets as and when the Council determines, a separate fund or funds as may be deemed necessary; and

(r) to further the interest of members in all legitimate ways and to employ funds of the Association as the Council may deem desirable for all objects and benefits included in the rules of the Association.

The Association provides indemnity payments for their members in respect of cancellation or suspension of their certificates or licences as follows:

(a) If a certificate or licence is cancelled by an official inquiry, then a payment equal to eighteen months basic salary (up to a maximum of £2500) is made to the member concerned.

(b) If a certificate or licence is suspended as the result of an official inquiry, monthly payments, equal to the member's salary (up to a maximum of £100 per month) will be paid. The number of such payments shall not exceed eight.

(c) If a lower grade of licence is granted as the result of an official inquiry, monthly payments equal to three-quarters of the member's salary at the time of the incident which gave rise to the official inquiry, will be made. No monthly payment may exceed £50 and the number of payments may not exceed eight.

(d) In the event of a member being ordered to pay a sum towards the costs of an official inquiry, the Association may reimburse the member up to a maximum of £1000.

If a member has to attend an official inquiry, the Association will arrange for legal representation and will pay reasonable legal costs. The Association will always pay reasonable legal costs even if the member is found guilty of some breach of discipline or of an offence against the law, but, in these cases, the Association will not make the indemnity payments described above.

The Association is controlled by its Council which consists of a President, Chairman, Vice-Chairman, General Secretary, three trustees and thirty full members of the Association. The Council consists of an equal number of navigating and engineer officers. Some of the powers of the Council may be delegated to a smaller Executive Committee but the bulk of the work connected with the day to day running of the Association falls on the shoulders of the General Secretary and his assistants. These assistants may be appointed to head office as National Secretaries, National Organizers, or as other specialized officials, or they may be appointed to serve at one of the eleven district offices in the major ports of the United Kingdom, or at Rotterdam.

For a comprehensive summary of the work done by the M.N.A.O.A., reference should be made to the Council's Report to the General Meeting. From this it will be seen that the Association is concerned with salaries, leaves and conditions; the prices and incomes policy; the Committee of Inquiry into Shipping; the Merchant Navy Officers' Pension Fund; safety; fire protection regulations; life-saving appliances rule; the grain regulations; health services for seafarers; training, qualifications and education; international conventions on load-lines and safety at sea; the Merchant Navy Welfare Board; and many other factors affecting the British shipping industry.

The Association is represented on a number of organizations, some of which are:

The Navigating and Engineering Panels of the National Maritime Board.

The Merchant Navy Welfare Board.

The Established Service Scheme.

The Merchant Navy Training Board.

Merchant Navy Officers' Pension Fund.

The Joint Maritime Commission, I.L.O.

Economic Development Committee for the Movement of Exports.

Standing Advisory Committee on the Carriage of Dangerous Goods and Explosives in Ships.

National Committee and Advisory Committee on Oil Pollution.

O.N.D. Joint Committee (Nautical Committee).

Council for National Academic Awards, Nautical Studies Board.

Seafarers' Education Service Commission.

Trinity House Joint Industrial Council.

As can be seen from all of the above, this Association is playing —and, in the future, will have to play—a major role in securing the prosperity of the Merchant Navy and of the country.

The Mercantile Marine Service Association

This Association was founded in 1857 and was incorporated by a special Act of Parliament in 1863. Its charter reads: "To conserve the interests of the British Merchant Navy; to promote the general improvement of nautical men by education and wholesome laws; to obtain redress of wrongs; to procure employment; to care for the helpless and aged; and by every possible means to seek the welfare of the Service."

Only two years after its formation, the M.M.S.A. obtained the frigate *Conway* and, in her, founded a nautical training establishment for boys. This establishment continued afloat for many years and was later transferred to buildings ashore. However, owing to the rising costs and changing patterns of training, the *Conway* is passing out of the control of the M.M.S.A. and Liverpool shipowners and is being taken over by the Cheshire Country Council and the British Shipping Federation.

In 1862 the M.M.S.A. set up a nautical school for those studying for certificates of competency (members of the Association were given free tuition but other students had to pay fees) and in 1880, the Association was granted the right of appeal against the findings of official Courts of Inquiry.

In 1882 the Association embarked on the charitable side of its charter by building a number of villas for aged Master Mariners and their wives. The M.M.S.A. is still actively engaged in this field of welfare and maintains a number of houses, bungalows and an infirmary for mariners and their widows. In addition, the Association administers a number of pension funds.

Originally, membership of the M.M.S.A. was open to all officers but, in 1942, it was decided to restrict membership to shipmasters only; officers interests were guarded by the Navigators and Engineer Officers' Union.

The present objects of the M.M.S.A. are:

(a) to unite in one association all shipmasters serving in command of British merchant ships;

(b) to improve the conditions of service of shipmasters and to promote the general interests of all members;

(c) to provide legal advice and assistance for members arising out of the practice of their profession;

(d) to join, or participate in the work or activities of, such national and international bodies as the Council may from time to time determine;

(e) to administer trusts, pension funds and residential establishments providing for the relief of distress among retired or necessitous British seafarers and their dependants.

The indemnity paid to members in respect of the cancellation or suspension of their certificates of competency or in respect of an order for costs against them is exactly the same as that paid to members of the Merchant Navy and Airline Officers' Association and, as that scale of indemnity payments has already been given under the heading of the M.N.A.O.A. it will not be repeated here.

The Mercantile Marine Service Association is controlled by a Council which consists of not less than forty nor more than fifty-three members. The M.M.S.A. has a full-time General Secretary and staff of officials to carry out the day-to-day administration of the Association's affairs.

The M.M.S.A. nominates representatives to the ship-masters' panel of the National Maritime Board and, in addition to this work, negotiates with shipowners on a number of problems affecting shipmasters, for example: improving conditions throughout the Merchant Navy; retirement and pension funds; crew accounts; carriage of wives; pilotage duties; rights of access to the top managers of shipping companies, and any other factors affecting their members. Like the other Associations and Unions, the M.M.S.A. is taking an active part in improving conditions at sea in order to improve the efficiency of the Merchant Navy.

The Radio Officers' Union

Although several attempts were made, between the years 1901 and 1912, to form an association or union of radio officers, the continuous existence of the present Radio Officers' Union dates from 1912. The R.O.U. is a registered trade union and is affiliated to the International Federation of Radio Officers, the British and Scottish Trade Union Congresses and the International Transport Workers Federation. Membership of the Union is very high and some 75 per cent of all radio officers at sea belong to the R.O.U.

This Union nominates the employees' representatives on the Radio Officers Panel of the N.M.B. and, in addition, negotiates with the radio companies and shipowners on improving conditions of service.

The objects of this Union are:

(a) to promote and extend the adoption of trade union principles, and to affiliate with such other trade unions and federations of trade unions, as in the opinion of the Executive Committee, may appear desirable;

(b) to promote, safeguard and watch over the interests of its members who are engaged in Radio Services, Cable Services and Telecommunication Services in all their branches;

(c) to protect and improve the conditions of service and the status of its members, and to endeavour to obtain for them reasonable hours of duty;

(d) to obtain salaries and allowances commensurate with the work and responsibilities of its members;

(e) to obtain improved accommodation for its members whilst engaged in the performance of their duties;

(f) to regulate the relations between its members and their employers and between employed persons *inter se*;

(g) to promote the social welfare of its members;

(h) to further or participate in any other action or purpose, financially or otherwise, or to do any other matter or thing which is not prohibited by law and is calculated, in the opinion of the Executive Committee, to further the interests of the Union or of the trade union movement generally;

(i) to secure, or assist in securing legislation and the effective administration of existing laws which affect the general and material welfare of its members as far as is permitted by law;

(j) the assistance of members and/or their dependants in cases of distressed circumstances;

(k) the payment of a sum of money on the death of any member;

(l) the insurance of the personal effects of its members;

(m) to affiliate with Foreign, Colonial or International Radio or Cable or other organizations, calculated, in the opinion of the Executive Committee, to advance the professional or general welfare of the members;

(n) to provide legal assistance to members in respect of matters arising out of or incidental to their employment;

(o) the protection of members in respect of unemployment and disputes; and

(p) for the purpose of furthering its objects, the Union may:
   (i) Establish District or Branch offices wherever and whenever found expedient;

(ii) Publish a newspaper or periodical of a non-political character.

The R.O.U. is governed by its Executive Committee and has a General Secretary and staff of officials, similar to that of the other Unions and Associations.

The Honourable Company of Master Mariners

The origin of the Company may be traced to the Annual Shipmasters' Dinner held in Liverpool on the 2nd March 1921 when Sir Robert Burton-Chadwick suggested that the profession was entitled to form, and was capable of forming, a Guild or Company very much on the lines of the old City of London Livery Companies. He envisaged, at that time, some such title as "The Worshipful Company of Shipmasters". As the outcome of his suggestion, Sir Robert was asked to make further enquiries in London, and he consulted many authorities. Thereafter the movement gathered strength, and, encouraged by the zeal of many earnest-minded seamen, found expression on the 25th June 1926 in the formation of the Company of Master Mariners.

The desire on the part of the Master Mariner for such a Company had been long cherished. Throughout the centuries he had seen the rise to fame and fortune of the great Livery Companies of London, while he, whose calling was steeped in traditions certainly as old as any other remained with neither Guild nor House.

The fact that in the twentieth century the Master Mariner should have found himself in such an unenviable position was not due to any reluctance on the part of the people to accord him the recognition he sought. The warmth and spontaneity of the welcome given to the Company at its inception, and emphasized since in such generous measure disprove such a theory. The reason undoubtedly lay in the exigencies of his calling, which kept him continually on the move and out of touch with public life. He found no opportunity to create for himself the representative body to which he aspired, and obviously no one else could create it for him. The effort had to come from the Service itself.

The hundred Master Mariners who comprised the Foundation Council of the Company were all men of long experience who had risen to high rank in their profession, both afloat and in executive positions ashore. They did not underestimate the magnitude of the task to which they had set their hands, and knew well how damaging to their profession as a whole would have been the consequence of failure. But they had faith in their ability to carry the Company to success, a faith which was abundantly justified by the enthusiasm with which the Company was acclaimed by the Service and the public. For themselves, as individuals, the Founders sought nothing; their aim was to create a Company which would endure as a worthy monument to the great traditions of their calling—a Company so constituted and administered as to draw to it the confidence of their fellow seamen, and one of which membership would be held a privilege.

The criticism has sometimes been voiced that because the membership of the Company is limited it is therefore exclusive, and further that a limited representation has no claim to be heard when other societies have memberships running into thousands. Such criticism is unjustified. Firstly, there is no element of exclusiveness in the membership, which is open to any Master Mariner who has held a certificate of competency as Master of a foreign-going ship, granted under the Merchant Shipping Acts, or a certificate of competency recognized as being of the same force as though so granted, for a minimum of five years immediately prior to the day on which he is proposed for membership. There is no other qualification. Secondly, the Company does not seek to encroach upon or enter into any sort of competition with the officers' societies whose excellent work is so well known and appreciated.

Its objects, briefly, are:

(1) To provide a central body representative of the senior officers of the Merchant Navy for the purpose of developing and promoting, in the interests of the Commonwealth, the traditions and efficiency of the British Merchant Navy as an Imperial Service;

(2) to encourage and maintain a high and honourable standard of ability and professional conduct in the officers of the Merchant Navy;

(3) to promote and maintain in all respects efficient and friendly co-operation between the Merchant Navy and the Royal Navy;

(4) to collect and distribute statistics and other information relating to the Merchant Navy or to nautical science;

(5) to constitute a body of experienced seamen, who will be available to act as members of, or to give evidence before, any Royal Commissions, Courts of Inquiry, Committees, or Boards of any description, or governing, examining or other bodies, official or otherwise, and who will be available for advice or consultation on all questions concerning or affecting the Merchant Navy, or judicial, commercial, scientific, educational or technical matters relating thereto;

(6) to provide facilities for the discussion and study of matters concerning or affecting the Merchant Navy, or sea-craft, navigation or nautical science;

(7) to provide a central consultative body of practical seamen, who will be available for information and advice on all matters connected with the safety and preservation of ships, passengers, seamen and cargo; and

(8) to provide in whole or in part for the maintenance of any necessitous Master Mariners and their dependants.

The Honourable Company's Livery Hall and headquarters are situated on board the *Wellington*—a sloop purchased from the Admiralty, and permanently berthed at Temple Stairs, Victoria Embankment, London, since December 1948.

The *Wellington* is the venue for the Company's annual conference for senior Merchant Navy officers, and for its informal meetings at which technical papers are read before members and invited guests, who frequently include officers studying in London for their certificates of competency. Many of the technical papers together with other matters of interest, are made available to members through the quarterly *Journal*[11]. Extracts from the

Journal are reprinted in booklet form as an occasional publication for wider distribution.

The Seafarers' Education Service

The Seafarers' Education Service was founded in 1919 as an offshoot of the Workers' Educational Association. It is a non-profit-making service, incorporated by Royal Charter. It is governed by a Commission representative of all facets of the shipping industry, government departments, and educational authorities. Full-time officers of the Service include a Director, Secretary and Librarian, and a total staff of about twenty-five.

The Service provides a first-class library service for merchant ships, paid for by shipowners. Sixteen hundred ships, the bulk of the Merchant Navy, are supplied with libraries and about 330,000 books are despatched each year. The Service spends about £40,000 a year on new books for these libraries. Libraries are changed twice a year mostly when ships call at United Kingdom ports. Depots are also maintained at 15 ports overseas, and ships are free to exchange libraries at these depots, or with each other. Individual seafarers may borrow books on free personal loan, while textbooks for professional studies may be hired.

The College of the Sea, a department of the Service, provides a tutorial form of course (by correspondence) for seafarers, in any subject not directly connected with their professional studies—it does not encroach upon the field of the nautical colleges. Subjects range from mathematics (about half the enrolments) to almost everything else. Students work at their own pace, and with or without an examination in view. For those who wish to take G.C.E. subjects, the College is an examination centre of the University of London, and examinations for this Board (and usually for the others as well) may normally be taken on board ship. Scholarship schemes are available for ratings of the deck and engineering departments who wish to study towards professional certificates.

For some years, the College has run a 16 mm film library service, used mainly to supplement theatrical films that shipowners have hired from commercial firms. Recently, tapes and films in other formats have been added to the film library service. The tapes started with language courses, and about twelve languages are now available, as well as tapes on the Collision Regulations, morse code, and various aspects of shipmaster's legal knowledge. Filmstrips and 8 mm loop films of nautical interest are being added to the library as they become available.

As well as its other functions, the Service is a registered bookseller. Book lists in particular subjects are available on demand, and these now include programmed texts. As teaching machines become available on board ship, the College expects to add a library of machine programmes to its existing libraries.

The journal of the Service, *The Seafarer*[21], is published quarterly, and costs 10/– per year. It contains articles of interest to seafarers concerning education, book reviews, and details of the annual competitions run by the Service in writing, poetry, art, handicraft and photography. Many an aspiring writer or artist has been encouraged by having his early work published in this journal.

More generally, the College of the Sea is a source of information for seafarers on any educational topic. If the College does not know the answer, then it can tell you who does.

The Merchant Navy Training Board

The Merchant Navy Training Board was established in 1935 with the main purpose of organizing an examination scheme for navigating cadets, under which cadets followed a standard syllabus of academic study at sea during their cadetship and were examined in it at the end of each of the first three years of their training at sea.

In more recent years there has been a growing awareness in the industry of the need for all seafarers to be systematically trained to perform their duties on board ship and to be encouraged to develop their full potential. There has also been an increasing appreciation of the need to have agreed policies for training and a greater degree of uniformity in similar courses throughout the country, without losing such flexibility as is necessary. It was agreed that this could best be done through a formal body representative of those mainly responsible for nautical training, and that the Merchant Navy Training Board should be reconstituted with wider terms of reference for this purpose.

Under its new constitution, the board keeps under its surveillance the whole field of the training and technical education of those making their career in the Merchant Navy. It considers ideas and opinions from all quarters on any training matter affecting the industry and gives its advice to the industry, to government departments, and to the education authorities on the training of Merchant Navy personnel.

The first meeting of the reconstituted board took place early in 1964, when it was agreed that there should be sections covering the training of deck officers, engineer officers and engine room ratings, deck ratings and catering personnel. Recently a radio officers' section has been formed.

The Pearson Report[20] commented favourably on the work of the M.N.T.B. in paragraph 34 of that report:

The Merchant Navy Training Board is entirely voluntary and is not a Training Board under the Industrial Training Act 1964 although it performs many of the functions of Boards set up under the Act in other industries. It has made very considerable progress in stimulating and co-ordinating training activities since it was re-constituted in 1964 and continuously reviews training arrangements in the light of changes in the way ships are designed and operated. We believe that it generally works well and effectively. Moreover, the Federation has been successful in ensuring that training costs are shared by shipping companies. The Federation itself bears half the cost of the National Sea Training Schools and meets the cost, either in whole or in part, of other training courses from levies required from members. In addition, rebates are made to companies which employ certain categories of newly recruited seamen and there is a per capita levy on all engineer officers to provide grants to companies which train engineer cadets.

The Pearson Report did, however, suggest that the shipping industry may come to appreciate the advantages a Statutory

Training Board could provide and that, should such a board be constituted, it would need to recognize the well-developed arrangements under which the Board of Trade organizes and supervises the examinations for certificates of competency.

Under its present constitution, the M.N.T.B. consists of representatives from shipowners, seafarers organizations, educational associations, and government departments. The M.N.T.B. is concerned with all the courses listed earlier in this chapter under the heading of "British Shipping Federation Courses" as well as the traditional and newer courses for seafarers held at colleges throughout the country.

The Marine Society

This society was founded in 1756 to ensure that no boy is prevented from going to sea because of lack of means. The society makes grants and loans towards meeting the cost of outfitting a boy. Bursaries are also available for boys, in need, to attend recognized pre-sea courses.

The Missions to Seamen

This is a Church of England society which provides clubs and other facilities for seafarers of all faiths. The society has clubs in most of the major ports of the world and local padres are always helpful in arranging sporting activities between different ships or between ship's and shore teams.

The Apostleship of the Sea

This Roman Catholic society provides clubs and facilities for seafarers of all faiths in ports throughout the world, the best known being their club, Atlantic House, in Liverpool.

CHAPTER 15

The Whole Man

IN AN article published some time ago[10], I developed a new way of visualizing a person. Let us now see if we can develop this concept still further in order to summarize the main points made in this book.

Each one of us has certain needs and urges, some of which are:

(a) the need to earn a living;
(b) the need for security in our prime groups, which can be described as the need for social contacts with—and acceptance by—others;
(c) the need for satisfaction in our jobs;
(d) the need for status, with which can be linked the urge to exert our self-importance;
(e) the need for self-respect;
(f) the need to know what is going on around us;
(g) the need to be appreciated;
(h) the need to keep physically fit;
(i) the need for some form of intellectual stimulation; and
(j) the need to engage in some form of creative activity.

Each one of us is able, with varying degrees of success, to satisfy some of these needs while the satisfaction of others depends, to large extent, on the actions of the people around us and, in particular, on the actions of our superiors. For example, (a) above is satisfied by learning a particular job; (b) by meeting people and making friends; (c) by being encouraged to give to our jobs a little more than we need to; (d) by developing our abilities in order to gain intrinsic status; (e) by being given—or by taking on—responsibilities; (f) by our superiors keeping us fully informed on all that is happening; (g) by our superiors taking an interest in us as whole, complete persons; (h) by participating in some sport or other; (i) by reading, studying or engaging in debate with others; and (j) by taking up a hobby, by making something or by developing new ways of operating our ships.

Let us now try to visualize a person as a sphere made up of a number of different planes; each plane representing that person's ability to satisfy a particular need.

When we talk of a well-rounded or well-balanced person, we mean that the radii of all these planes are of equal size. Figure 15.1 illustrates this concept for an average boy who has just left school and has embarked on a career at sea. Let us assume, for a moment, that his academic knowledge, his sporting and social abilities, his satisfaction and pride in the job he has chosen, his self-respect, and his creative ability are at much the same standard. The radii of all the various planes will be equal and these planes could be visualized as forming the sphere shown in the figure. I am quite aware that the needs, urges and abilities fall into different psychological categories and that strong interest or motivation may make one plane larger than the others: one boy may be an outstanding sportsman, another may be a brilliant mathematician, while still another may have interest in girls as his dominant trait. In all these cases, the relevant plane in each boy's make up will be extended. On the other hand, we may have a boy who is hopeless at sport, or one whose academic standard is very low, or still another whose shyness prevents him from establishing normal social contacts with others. In these cases, the relevant plane in each boy's make-up will be reduced. The development of this concept will, however, be confined to men of average all-round ability. The most important point is to trace the development of the size of each plane during the boy's —or man's—years at sea.

If we are going to keep this boy a well-rounded person, we must ensure that all the planes grow at much the same rate for, if some of these planes grow while others diminish, we will end

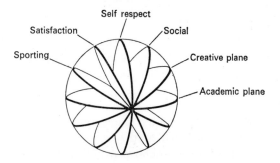

FIG. 15.1. A concept of a young, well-balanced boy just embarking on his sea career.

up with an unbalanced man who, while being perfectly competent in some fields of activity, is unable to satisfy many of his needs. Such a man is not a very happy person and not only may he be inefficient in some aspects of his job but his unhappiness may cause him to leave the sea at an early age or cause him to spread discontent among his associates aboard ship.

As was said earlier, Fig. 15.1 illustrates a boy's make-up at the beginning of his sea career. As a result of the technical and academic training he receives in his nautical school and aboard ship, his academic plane will grow into a zone of general nautical knowledge and, after further years at sea, it may be described as

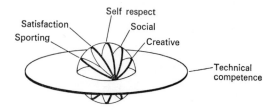

FIG. 15.2. A concept of man who has spent years developing his technical competence without developing the other planes in his make-up. Note how his sporting, social and creative planes, etc., are smaller than when he first went to sea.

a zone of technical competence. If, while he is acquiring this technical knowledge, he neglects his sporting, social and creative needs and abilities and if, during this time, his superiors suppress his initiative, give him no responsibility, and do not appreciate his efforts (thus lowering his self-respect), all those planes may diminish until they are smaller than when he first went to sea. His resultant make-up is illustrated in Fig. 15.2, and in no way could he be called a "rounded" or well-balanced man.

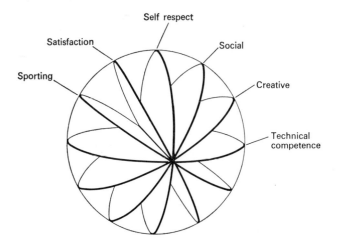

FIG. 15.3. The "Whole Man". All his planes are the same size: he is a bigger and better man than when he first went to sea.

Let each one of us, therefore, pay attention to all our planes in order to make ourselves well-balanced, rounded men and let those of us who are managing men at sea be conscious of our duty to help them grow into well-rounded men, much larger in all respects than when they first went to sea. Whenever we can, let us encourage their participation in sporting and social activities as described in the chapter on Crew Welfare, let us encourage them to pursue their academic studies, let us encourage them to give all they can to their jobs and, most important of all, let us increase their plane of self-respect by appreciating their efforts, by giving them responsibilities, by keeping them fully informed on all that is happening, and by recognizing them as whole, complete persons.

If you have just finished reading this book aboard a ship and are just about to go out on deck to issue an instruction or reprimand to someone, or if you finished reading it in an office and you are just about to interview a man in connection with his service in his last ship, say to yourself, "How can I help this man to grow into a bigger and better man than he is at present? How can I help him to keep his dignity?"

References

1. *The Chain Testers' Handbook.* Chain Testers' Association.
2. *Denholm News.* J. & J. Denholm Ltd.
3. *Working with Denholms.* J. & J. Denholm Ltd.
4. ELDEN, R. *Ship Management.* Cornell Maritime Press.
5. HOPE, Dr. R. *Spare Time at Sea.* S.E.S.
6. HOPE, Dr. R. *A Shore-goer's Guide to World Ports.* Maritime Press.
7. Industrial Training Act, 1964. H.M.S.O.
8. *Safety in Dock Work.* International Labour Office.
9. *Journal of Commerce*, 8 and 15 November 1967.
10. *Journal of Commerce Annual Review*, 1967.
11. *Journal of the Honourable Company of Master Mariners.*
12. *Lloyd's List*, 8 and 15 November 1967.
13. Merchant Shipping Act, 1894. H.M.S.O.
14. *National Maritime Board Year Book.* N.M.B.
15. *Shipboard Handbook.* National Union of Seamen N.U.S.
16. Ramsey, R. A. *Managers and Men.* Ure Smith.
17. Report of the Central Advisory Committee for Education (England). (Newsom Report). H.M.S.O.
18. Report of the Department of Education and Science. Cmnd. 3226 H.M.S.O.
19. Report on Higher Education. (Robbins.Report) Cmnd.2154. H.M.S.O.
20. Final Report of the Court of Inquiry into certain matters concerning the Shipping Industry. (Pearson Report). Cmnd. 3211. H.M.S.O.
21. *The Seafarer.* Seafarers' Education Service. S.E.S.
22. *Shipping World and Shipbuilder*, 18 January 1968.

References 7, 13, 17, 18, 19 and 20 are published with the permission of the Controller of Her Majesty's Stationery Office.

Index